High Finance: The Secrets Wall Street Doesn't Want You to Know

Copyright © 2016, North of Sunset Publishing

This book is dedicated to Dennis, Lisa, Brian, Howard, Nick, and Darah—my first six clients. Thank you all for taking a chance on me.

Table of Contents

Preface—My Best (Worst) Trade

In January of 2015, I was a 19-year old freshman at the University of Miami. Then and there, I made the biggest trade of my life, and at one point I was down about 25,000 dollars. Apple had just released the iPhone 6, and I absolutely knew it was a bigger hit than Wall Street thought it was. I went out into the options market to bet basically all the money I had ever made in stocks, about 40,000 dollars, on Apple rising more than 4 percent in 30 days, with an all important earnings report in the middle of the 30 days. I purchased the right to buy 10,000 shares at 115 dollars a share, giving me control of about 1.15 million dollars in Apple stock. I had done about 100 hours of research on every aspect of Apple, from the supply chain, to cash flow, to how many shares Apple would buy back that quarter.

I bet that Apple's earnings report would be spectacular, and if I were wrong, I would have lost all the profit I had ever made in stocks, over six years of work in one bad trade. My entire family was texting me every day with updates on Apple's stock price. I ended up being 100 percent right, Apple crushed analysts expectations, going up 18 points in 2 ½ weeks to 133 a share by the expiration of my options, at which point the position was worth nearly 200,000 dollars. Only catch was, I psyched myself out and got scared when I was up about 20,000 after earnings, and I sold it. That's trading for you.

Trading is hard, but also extremely rewarding. I quit trading for such high stakes after that crash course in risk management. After that trade, I went back to the drawing board to see how I could get good returns with low risk, and I converted to more of an investing mindset, following simple, solid methods to make money without pulling my hair out. I always managed money more conservatively for my clients, but I tended to trade extremely aggressively for myself. My punishment for being such a reckless trader? None. I got away with it, walking away with quite a bit of trading profit over the years, but I knew I needed to change. I want to share my knowledge in investing and trading, so you can imitate my success. I also want you to learn from my mistakes, so you don't have to make them too. Wall Street lays a lot of traps to separate

you from your money. I'll map them out for you so you know where

Wall Street's minefields are and can avoid them.

Introduction

I was the kind of kid who went to the principal's office a lot. My mom says I went 14 times in middle school alone. My mom even had a special alarm bell ringtone on her phone for the principal's office. You could say I was just the class clown, but I think I just saw the world a little differently. Even at a young age, I couldn't help but play the angles to make money. One day, my mom got a phone call from Mrs. Bradley, my middle school principal (I started off as one of her least favorite students, but after a lot of detentions and visits, she and her secretary really grew to like me). "Logan is loan sharking," she told my mom. "What???" my mom replied. "Yes, he's charging usurious interest rates to the other children for snack money," the principal said. "I'll talk to him," my mom said with a sigh.

Every Friday we had smoothie day at school. Middle schoolers being middle schoolers, a good amount of kids would not have the 2 dollars in cash on them to buy their smoothie. That's where I stepped in. I would loan 2 dollars to people, but they would have to pay me back 3 dollars on Monday (4 bucks if I didn't like them). Like any wannabe Mafioso, if they didn't pay me Monday, I would tack on additional interest. I think I collected 8 dollars in interest from some redheaded kid on a 2-dollar debt; he was probably the one who told the principal. My mom sat me down and lectured me, but my dad and grandpa applauded me. When my grandpa found out it, it absolutely made his year. To this day, it comes up nearly every time the family gets together, and everyone has a good laugh.

I graduated from middle school loan sharking into investing, and started trading within a short period after that. I quickly picked up 2 clients in my neighborhood, getting an incredibly generous 50 percent of the profits. I bought a car with my profits before I could even legally drive it. I really threw myself into understanding everything about markets that I could at a very young age. I got in plenty of trouble along the way, nothing serious, but trouble nonetheless, and I learned more about myself and about the markets than I thought was possible. I want to share my experiences investing and trading, so you not only can repeat my successes, but so you don't have to learn all my mistakes the hard way.

Basically, there are three ways to make money investing, and I am devoting a section to each of them, plus a fourth for managing taxes and asset protection. The three ways to make money investing are:

1.   Have equity in a business. Despite my smoothie loan sharking adventures, investing in equities is the conventional way to invest money for a decent return. This includes owning a business or a piece in a business (private equity), or stocks. Private equity sounds fancy, but all it really involves is investing in a private business. I didn't highlight it in the story, but the smoothie guy that packed 100ish smoothies in a cooler and sold them on Fridays probably made 60-70 percent of his revenue as profit, essentially making 120 bucks for

an hour or so of work. The stock market is misunderstood, but it really just comes down to providing capital for businesses, and getting a cut of the profit in return.

2.   Debt. Whether it's lending money to kids for smoothies or lending money to the US government to finance their latest nonsense, *there is always more demand for money than there is supply.* When there is always more demand than supply, lenders make money. For example, credit card lending is one of the most profitable businesses in the United States, ever. Most financial advisors recommend keeping anywhere from 20 to 60 percent of your investing assets in bonds, and I think this is one of their only solid pieces of advice. I think it is always advisable to allocate some cash to bonds, especially if you have

substantial assets, but the rise of fintech and peer to peer lending gives you the ability to cut out the middleman and get a direct piece of the lending action, without the downside risk of the stock market. Everyone knows that the casinos in Las Vegas rake it in from their patrons, but behind the scenes, the real flow of cash goes to the people who own the junk bonds that financed the casinos. If the casinos don't make the huge interest payments, the bondholders take the keys.

3. Wagering/Trading. Imagine I let kids go double or nothing on their smoothie debts, but charged them a dollar for the privilege of betting. Assuming I could collect it, I would make money on average. The word wagering might make you think of casinos, but the largest takers of bets, in a way, are insurance companies. When you buy

insurance, you are essentially betting that something will go wrong, and the insurance company is betting that things will go right. Trading stocks falls under the category of wagering too. It is smart to bet if you have the advantage and control risk, but otherwise betting is destructive to your wealth. Casinos are excellent examples of places not to bet.

Part 1: Equity Investment

Understanding The Market

Wall Street wants you to think that finance is such a great

mystery that you have to get an MBA and work in an investment

bank to even begin to understand it. They want you to think that

the only way to grow your wealth is to hand it over to them and let

them charge you hefty fees for their sacred knowledge of how to

manage your hard earned cash. They use the biggest words they

can think of, and hand unnecessarily thick prospectuses to every

potential investor filled with nonsense legalese to make investors think that they are the only ones who can possibly understand what is going on. At the same time, they charge all kinds of fees to pay for their quarterly Caribbean getaways and Gucci loafers that never get scuffed. They don't want you to know this, but knowledge of finance is within the reach of the average person. Wall Street chooses not to educate you, because they want to take your money away from you.

Wall Street especially loves to feed off of affluent professionals with plenty of money to invest that Wall Street can siphon away. The vast majority of highly educated, high earning Americans aren't in Wall Street's scams. In fact, they are the biggest victims. The financial knowledge gap between high earners and everyone else isn't as big as you would think. High earners are better than most, but often don't have a good understanding of finance. The top percentiles of income earners in this country usually don't get there by financial wizardry, but by hard work and dedication. The largest group of people in the top five percent of income earners are actually doctors. Other high earners are mostly professionals, such as lawyers and corporate executives. (Athletes and entertainers are only a rounding error in the American wealth picture). The lack of financial knowledge among high earning people is truly shocking. Doctors in particular are notorious for running into financial trouble despite high incomes. If the highest income earners in the country know so little about investing and finance, how hard are things for those who aren't in that income bracket? It is even harder for those who aren't high-income earners. Everyone has goals, and I think they should have a fair shot to achieve them. The ability to make a better life for your family is what the United States of America was founded on, and lack of Wall Street knowledge shouldn't stand in the way. The main problem with stock brokers, financial advisors, fund managers, etc., is that they make it harder for you to achieve your goals. They make money off of fees and commissions, which is inherently a conflict of interest— they eat a slice of your pie, you have less pie. In a day in age when there are ETFs charging 0.07 percent per year on your money that track the market perfectly, financial advisors are being paid 2.5

percent sales charges to place client money in mediocre funds charging 1 percent per year. Most mutual fund managers can't beat the market if their lives depended on it, consistently failing to deliver on their promises. I'm not going to sit here and tell you I can easily make you a multimillionaire investing with a 50,000 salary, because that is not true. What I can do for you is show you how the game really works, what the rules are, and how you can benefit from it. Your ability to accumulate cash is going to be proportional to your ability to earn it, but you can greatly accelerate the process.

That said, not everyone who earns good money does so by spending their 20s in medical school and specializing in knee injuries in a ski town, although that is a highly bankable career path. The rest of the top income earners who aren't doctors and lawyers are mostly business owners and their heirs, with a few other finance oriented people who know how the game is played– wealthy traders and investors. Learn the secrets, and prosper, or ignore them and flounder. Just how bad is the lack of knowledge of finance among the average person?

According to the Federal Reserve numbers published in 2015, only 48 percent of Americans have any stock or bond investments, including mandatory 401(k) stock contributions.

Additionally:

- Only 1 in 7 people invest in stocks or ETFs outside of mutual funds or employer sponsored accounts.

- Only 1 in 9 have stocks outside of a retirement account.

- 1 in 100 own real estate other than their house

- Mean credit card debt- 12,000 dollars- corresponds to roughly 1800 dollars in interest per household assuming a 15 percent interest rate. Most households don't have credit card debt but those who do... Scary.

- Average home equity- less than 50 percent

- Percentage of people who incorporate their businesses in LLCs- less than 10 percent.

This lack of knowledge really isn't the fault of the people who don't invest. The problem is with the system at large. They don't teach you how to invest a bonus check or inheritance or how to manage a credit card bill in school, and Wall Street just wants to steal your money. I have made six figures trading stocks in between my clients and myself, and I know pretty much every trick in the book. I will break them down for you to the best of my ability, in language you can understand. If you're reading this, I know you are already smarter than average, and finance really isn't that complicated anyway.

The stock market is accessible to anyone who wants to play. Over the short and long term, it tends to be a profitable endeavor. It doesn't matter if you are a 45-year-old ex-con or a 13-year-old finance aficionado, the market is open and you can sell and withdraw your profits whenever you please. If you would like to have more money, opening an online brokerage account is an excellent idea. Just by finding some regular money to deposit, you can start setting the age-old profit machine in motion and begin cultivating your empire. Most financial gurus only endorse long-term investment, but I am actually going to go out on a limb here and say that is too restrictive to tell people that they can't touch their money for years or decades. Even if your account balance grows exponentially with time, time is a more valuable commodity than money. *Many people look at the stock market like a time machine that they can't touch for 20 years or until they retire, and I think this thinking needs to be challenged.* Wall Street promotes this explanation, because if you invest with them for the long term, they make their hefty fees, year after year, and the profitability of the stock market means you won't even notice all the missing money. Nobody is forcing you to pay all these fees though, and you won't if you follow my advice. Let's get a working understanding of the stock market first, because watching CNBC can feel like watching a casino floor, even to experienced investors. Understanding probabilities is the key to understanding the market; it takes the noise away from the truth.

What are the odds are of the stock market going up on any given day?

From 1950 to 2016, the stock market rose on 53.6 percent of days, and fell on 46.4 percent of days. That's better than a 50 percent chance of making money on any given day! You should be more comfortable putting money in the broad market for short periods of time, assuming you can tolerate risking a loss. The only catch is that the market tends to take the stairs up and the elevator down, so to speak. That means, in practical terms, that when the market rises, which it does most of the time, it goes up slow, and when it falls, it tends to fall fast. Still, the stock market has a strong tendency to go up over time, as you will see.

What are the odds of the market going up for the year?

The odds of the market rising for any given year are roughly 75-80 percent, when accounting for dividends. With such good odds for success, there is no reason to be excessively afraid of the stock market. The 2008 financial crisis caused a lot of people to swear off

20

stocks, but the market came back quickly from its bear market low. The takeaway here is that if you have extra money that you don't immediately need to spend, your odds of being able to cash out for more in a few months are higher than you think. In fact, the market goes up over 60 percent of months, and about 70 percent of 3-month periods. *It is okay to be in the market for shorter periods of time, chances are you will profit.* However if markets go down, you may do well to wait until they come back up to sell, or come to terms with the fact that you made a statistically winning decision, but one that doesn't always work out perfectly, and sell. It is popular to the point of being cliché to say that you are a long-term investor, but you aren't screwing yourself by holding for a few weeks or months. Get a big bonus or other decent sized check and plan on spending it in a few months? Toss it in the market; odds are you will make a profit when you sell. These odds of success are for the broad market as a whole, which you can access through any low cost Vanguard ETF. If you only invest in one or two stocks, you have more potential risk, and it's not as much of a layup. I actually want to encourage short term investing as much as possible. If you want to do stocks, and you want to cash out in 3 months or 6 months, that is perfectly fine. Especially if you are just starting out and want to see how you feel about it, or if you are younger and want to use the profit for something cool, the odds are in your favor. Trading is something that you shouldn't do if you aren't experienced, but I think that short term investing has an unnecessarily bad reputation. Everyone says they want to be in things for the long term, but things come up all the time that disrupt long term plans.

The odds of an up year in the market are about 80 percent, but how about longer periods of time? The news is even better! The longer you are in the market, the more you allow the return component of your investment to dominate the risk part of your investment. *Barring a zombie apocalypse, over a long enough period, your odds of making money in stocks converge with 100 percent.* What the gurus get wrong isn't that short term investing is dumb; it's just that long term investing is even better. Over a 10 year period, the worst you could do if you bought any time in the last century was to do a little better than break even, even if you bought right before a crash. Long term investing is more guaranteed to succeed, and also benefits from favorable tax treatment of capital gains and dividends, and investing for a long enough time gives you odds of near 100 percent chance of profit. Only downside is the fact that it takes a lot of time to get there. The upside to both styles is whatever wealth you have at your disposal can be used to make you even more money.

The stock market is all about risk and return, and so far, we have mostly discussed the return. What is the risk, however? The main risk of the market at large is the fluctuation in the value of stocks. Buy before a correction, and you could only be able to sell for about 90 cents per dollar you invested, if you choose to sell then. Buy before a bear market or crash, and you could have 70-80 cents on the dollar. The market crashed even further in 2008, but crashes of that magnitude are fairly rare, and don't usually last a long time.

What can investors expect when investing in stocks? Corrections, defined as stock prices falling 10 percent or more from peak to trough, happen fairly often. The market will fall 10 percent at some point, peak to trough, approximately once per year. On average, when this happens, the market falls roughly 13 percent (Reading in between the lines here shows that most corrections aren't much deeper than 10 percent). After a correction, it usually takes 3 months for the market to recover the losses. A lot of investors think that stocks go straight up, which is false, but even more investors are far too pessimistic and think that the market crashes all the time. People consistently overestimate the odds of market crashes, over both short and longer periods of time. The best way to handle corrections is to be patient if you are caught in one and think of investing in markets in terms of probabilities.

Bear markets, on the other hand, are different animals than corrections. They happen, on average, roughly every 7 years, and result in the market falling from 20-35 percent (2008 was about -45 percent). Unlike corrections, bear markets tend to be caused by economic recessions, when the earnings of companies fall significantly, even resulting in (mostly) temporary losses for vulnerable sectors. Losses threaten the ability of companies to meet their obligations, and companies that lose money for a long enough time go bankrupt, leaving their shareholders with worthless paper. Bear markets tend to last longer than corrections, and the market will fall for a year or two during these times. It usually takes 3-4 years for the market to recover its all time high set before the bear market. Don't worry, however. I can show you how to handle and sometimes even avoid bear markets, and how to navigate any market environment to produce profits.

Bear markets tend to be caused by one of three things, oil shocks, high valuations, and economic recessions. Oil shocks are the easiest to spot. If the price of oil spikes high enough (oil hit 147 dollars a barrel in 2008), it will have a strong negative effect on corporate profits, and economic growth. The economy was already fragile in 2008, and when oil spiked in the spring and summer of that year, smart investors shifted into bonds. High prices at the pump directly take money out of consumer's pockets, making it harder for them to do everything from making their mortgage payments to spending money in the retail sector and on new technology. *Any time the price of oil spikes to a level that causes pain to the American consumer; you want to shift some money into safer investments, like bonds.* Some pundits worry about inflation caused by rising oil prices, but I think that high oil prices have little effect on inflation since they tend to reduce consumer spending.

High valuations/high interest rates are another bear market precedent. US stock markets traded for record multiples in the late 1990s, before underperforming for nearly a decade. Japanese stock markets reached record heights in 1989, and have not recovered that price level since, although dividends have put investors back in the black there. The consequences of overpaying for the broad market as a whole tend to be milder, resulting in below average returns rather than outright losses. However, what you want to watch out for is sectors getting too hot. US technology stocks traded at ridiculous multiples in the late 1990s, setting investor expectations far too high. When investors readjusted their expectations, tech stocks dropped like they had cement shoes. At the same time the tech bubble in the 1990s occurred, the fed hiked interest rates, culminating in raising short-term interest rates to 5.75 percent in February 2000. The smart money slid into the safety of bonds for a guaranteed 6-7 percent return, while the Wall Street promotion machine continued to pull gullible investors into buying worthless Internet stocks, losing the public billions of dollars. You want to invest in growth, but not at any price. Low interest rates tend to support higher stock valuations, but as interest rates rise, stock valuations fall. Orienting your investment dollars towards cash flow and solid performance helps you win by avoiding drastically overpaying for earnings.

The last cause of bear markets is the only risk that I really don't know how to avoid, and that is when the economy slides into recession. The terrorist attacks of September 11, 2001 and the 2008 financial crisis punished stock investors, and neither was predicted ahead of time with any accuracy. The economy historically tends to go in cycles of strong economic growth followed by periods of brief correction/contraction. Bear markets almost always coincide with recessions, and many recessions sneak up on investors and economists. There is an old joke about economists predicting 8 of the last 3 recessions, and the answer is that no one really knows exactly when the economy will slow down. The best defense is really to position your portfolio to weather any storm that the market might throw at it, and know that the odds are in your favor. Bear markets caused by recession present great opportunities to buy stocks, and you can often double your money in 3-4 years by buying in times of turmoil.

Cash Flow is King

We know that stocks go up over time, but why? Wall Street and its army of brokers and advisors want you to think it is the most complicated thing ever, but in reality it is quite simple. Stocks go up over time because they are technically pieces of businesses, and businesses make money. So, if you invest in Wal-Mart, every time someone checks out at any Wal-Mart store, they pay for their stuff, the money goes into the cash register, and at the end of the day, all the money in the Wal-Mart goes to the bank, where it is deposited. This money is first used to pay expenses, but everything after is profit. At the end of each quarter, Wal-Mart takes either takes this profit and sends checks to every shareholder in the company (Dividends), or invests them back in the company to grow earnings more (Buybacks, Capital Expenditures). It turns out, in 2015, Wal-Mart paid about 40 percent of its profits in dividends, which resulted in checks being sent to every shareholder. As profits go up, companies raise their dividends to match their desired payout ratio. Also, companies treat dividends as sacred, and will cut costs as aggressively as they need to protect the dividend in tough times. The other 60 percent of the profit is used for a combination of share buybacks (buying shares on the open market and retiring them, which effectively reduces the number of shareholders so fewer people have to split the pie), and capital expenditures (usually opening new stores).

There are only two ways you can make money in stocks. You can get dividends, which are awesome—I always smile when I get mine, or sell your shares for more than you paid, which is a capital gain— I usually shout at my computer when I get those. You will be able to sell shares for more than you paid because the earnings of the company have grown, or because people are willing to accept a lower return in the future. Depending on what kind of stocks you buy, dividends are typically going to represent about 30-40 percent of your returns, and capital gains are typically going to be 60-70 percent. Additionally, you can use your dividends to buy even more stock, which exponentially grows your money. When you get even more dividends from shares you bought with last month's dividends, it's like getting interest on interest, but even better.

Stock Returns

Another question new and seasoned investors ask is, "What return can I expect from investing in stocks?" Don't feel bad about this, because the highest paid people in finance also ask each other this question all day long. I actually have a simple answer for this, and you can adjust it based on my assumptions. Your average returns from a stock can be broken down into a simple formula. **Percentage Return= Earnings Yield + Growth.** The earnings yield is simply the earnings divided by the share price, expressed as a percentage (1/ Price to Earnings Ratio, for those more finance oriented). The talking heads on TV love to talk about multiples, which is what they mean when they say, "The market is expensive," or, "Stocks are cheap." So, for example, if Wal-Mart (WMT) is trading for 70 dollars a share, and its earnings are 4.5 dollars a share, its earnings yield is 6.45 percent. For every 70 you throw in, you make 4.5 per year. Therefore, WMT has base return of 6.45 percent per year. The second part of the equation, however is to account for the growth. Wal-Mart should grow at about the same pace as the US economy, unless they want to put a Wal-Mart in every neighborhood, which is probably not the best use of cash. So, add 3 percent to the 6.45, and you get 9.45 percent. Now, we can't be 100 percent sure that WMT is a great investment, but 9.45 percent is a pretty strong return. Therefore, we can say that it's a good investment. The earnings yield of the market at large is typically between 5-6 percent, and earnings growth averages about 3 percent, so the average return of stocks is around 8-9 percent. The intelligentsia academic types you see on CNBC confuse this with the GDP growth rate, and say that the market can't go up faster than GDP. They are wrong, because they are confusing the growth of the output with the output of the economy itself. *Remember, the stock market averages a positive return of earnings yield plus growth.* You can also calculate this for sectors, and determine which sectors of the market to invest in. Utilities, for example are expensive, and can't grow faster than GDP due to government regulation their returns are in the 5-6 percent range (you wouldn't want your electric bill to grow faster anyway). They also have large amounts of debt they have to service, which creates the risk that they can't pay their obligations, leaving shareholders to hold the bag. Technology companies, on the other hand, have an earnings yield of 5-6 percent, and growth prospects faster than GDP–3-4 percent. Technology companies return roughly 9-10 percent on investment. For the money, you are best off investing in the technology sector, which has lots of growth, and not a lot of debt. Health care is also good, but somewhat trickier due to the potential government influence on profits. Still, health care is one of the better sectors to invest in. There is nothing wrong with picking sectors instead of spending large amounts of time analyzing stocks. The increased diversification will also help you reduce risk and increase profit. In fact, diversification is crucially important to successful investing, because it increases returns and decreases risk at the same time.

Remember my explanation of bear markets? Those normally happen because the earnings of companies fall in a recession. When the earnings of companies fall, people won't pay as much for stocks, because they need a lower price to get the same earnings

yield. If problems are related to the economic conditions at the

time, and not bad management, prices will recover in a year or two.

Fortunately, unless you borrowed money to buy the stock, no one

will force you to sell into a bad market, and patient investors usually

become rich investors. The average returns for stock and bond

markets:

S&P 500 Index (1944-2014)

Average Annual Return- 7.53 price appreciation plus dividends
(roughly 3 percent)-10.54 percent

Annual Standard Deviation- 16.5 percent- (Two thirds of years show
returns between -6 percent and +26 percent, positive roughly 75-80
percent of years)

Investment Grade Bonds

Average Return- 5.5 percent (1926-2014)

Standard Deviation- 4.6 percent (1926-2014) (80-85 percent of
years positive in bonds)

These are the mean returns from stocks and bonds over the

last 70 years. I expect returns to be somewhat lower in the future

for both stocks and bonds, due to two reasons. The first reason is

that bonds don't pay as much interest as they did back in the old days when interest rates were over 10 percent. The second reason

is a little more complicated, and it is that the arithmetic mean,

which I put above, is different from the geometric mean. *Geometric*

mean is what you actually earn if you invest a lump sum in the stock

market, which is not the same as adding up the returns for every

year and dividing by the number of years. The reason why is this. If

you have a 100-dollar investment that goes down 50 percent one

year and goes up 50 percent the next year, you only have 75 dollars.

Year 1- $100*.5=50$ Year 2- $50*1.5=75$. Your average (arithmetic)

return is 0 percent. However, you only have 75 dollars. Your return

in the real world is -25 percent. Arithmetic mean assumes that you

have the same starting balance every year, so if you lose money,

you have to top it up to your original amount to get the "average"

return. However, if you regularly contribute to an investment

account, your return will be somewhere in between the geometric

mean and arithmetic mean.

I'm going to take a quick sidebar here to highlight another

Wall Street scam. This particular scam is leveraged ETFs. ETFs are normally good, safe wealth management tools, but leveraged ETFs

are like the evil stepbrother to the Vanguard ETFs that are so good

for building wealth. Leveraged ETFs are scams, and people lose

money to them all the time. In the case of the double and triple

long funds, it technically says in the prospectus that they should

only be held for a day or two, but this is not what most investors

do, and they don't know the issue, because in a calm and up

trending market, the ETFs outperform the market. The problem

with leveraged ETFs is that they triple the *daily* performance of

whatever they are supposed to track, not the long-term

performance. So, when the market goes down 10 percent, they go

down 30. When the market goes back up 10 percent, they get back

21. Because they have to rebalance daily, they lose money to

slippage in choppy markets. The next time markets have a sharp

downturn; all of these ETFs will show 90 percent plus losses. Then,

the issuer will close the fund after the bear market, which every

issuer did after 2008, and make a new fund with a similar name, but

without the incriminating graph showing the leveraged ETF going to zero. Wall Street does this for mutual funds too; they close down funds that underperform, and keep the ones open that outperform, so investors think that all their funds are winners. All the while, they pocket 1 percent +/- fees on every dime invested with them, and advertise them as "a great tool for traders," with a small print blurb at the bottom in which translates to English from legalese as "thanks for letting us steal your money, have a nice day." Don't invest in leveraged ETFs; one day, you'll be happy you didn't. Instead, design your investment portfolio using tried and true methods to build your wealth.

Under The Hood of a Well-Designed Investment Portfolio

The mechanics of a well-designed investment portfolio are fairly simple; they rely on investments that pay dividends, rents, interest or any cash flow. This works out so that if you earn 5 percent on your investments, which is very conservative, then *every dollar in assets you have will earn you 5 cents in income per year.* This is the golden rule of finance, that every dollar you have is a soldier, and that soldier's job is to put a nickel in your pocket, every year, for eternity. I actually think it's fairly easy to do better than that without taking extra risk. Lots of mothers like to tell their children that money doesn't grow on trees, but that actually isn't true if you are wealthy and have a well-designed investment portfolio. If you can get your hands on a million dollars, you can usually get about 50,000 dollars per year in income for life, without even cracking a sweat, or making any withdrawals from your million dollars. If you have 10 million, that's 500,000 per year. This is dividend and interest income, much of it taxed at half the normal rate, or tax-free. In addition to the passive income, you will make money roughly 75-80 percent of years from capital gains, usually more than your dividends, even if the gains are somewhat unpredictable. Dividends are the cake, and capital gains are the icing. You can even invest in municipal bonds, which pay interest that is 100 percent tax-free. This simple setup is responsible for a lot of really nice vacation homes and people who get to play golf every day.

Why Fees are Bad

Letting someone charge you 1-2 percent a year to manage your money doesn't seem like a terrible idea at first glance. However, it is guaranteed to reduce your investment return by whatever fee they charge. No finance book would be complete without an ode to compound interest, so here is a graph of your return on a 100,000-dollar investment at a return of 7.5 percent per year, which is a solid, achievable return figure.

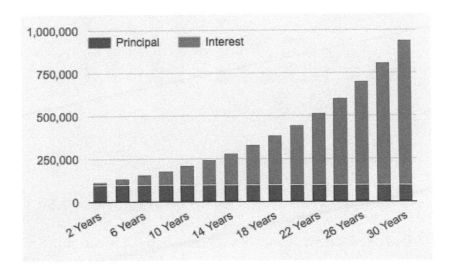

After 30 years, if you don't touch the principal and earn a 7.5 percent return, you have about 942,000 dollars in your portfolio. This is a very solid return, and you can make it in your sleep with some simple, solid financial principles. Earning over 9 times initial

return on your investment will make your financial life a lot better,

no matter how rich you are. The next graph is with 1.5 percent per

year in fees taken out, by paying an advisor 1 percent, and average

mutual fund cost of about 0.5 percent.

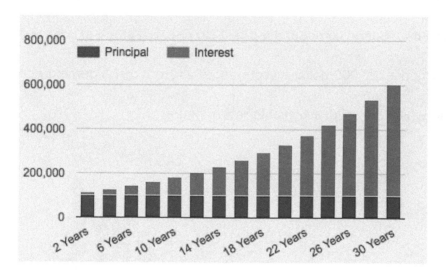

Instead of having 942,000 dollars in assets like before, we have a

balance of about 602,000 dollars when we are being hit with 1.5

percent fees per year. You could buy a house in most areas of the

United States with the difference in portfolio value. *If you had*

started with a million dollar investment, the difference in portfolio

value is over 3 million dollars. That money goes straight into your financial advisors pocket, so he can buy fancy cars and take nice vacations. You need to fire your financial advisor, and you need to take control of your financial future, the cost of ignorance is simply too high. Most financial advisors just do exactly what I am telling you to do, but charge you hefty fees to do it. You also need to move your money out of expensive mutual funds and into passively managed index funds. 65 percent of mutual managers underperform the market in any given year, and as many as 80 percent underperform the market over a 10 year period. As I said before, the mutual fund companies close down the underperforming funds and roll them into new funds so they can rinse and repeat, raking in the cash the whole time. This is just another example of how Wall Street and the financial industry don't have your best interest in mind; they have their own interests in mind instead.

Rules for Investing in Stocks

If you are well versed in the stock market, congratulations! If you are not so well versed, then read this section twice, because it shows various ways the market can hurt you and how to avoid them. Learn from my mistakes, so you don't have to experience them yourself.

1. Choose the right broker. When choosing a broker, there is really only one thing you should think about. That thing is the commission your broker charges. Think commissions aren't important? They are. The reason why is paying commission makes you poorer whether you are great at investing or terrible. By the time I turned 19, I had paid over 10,000 dollars in commission from trading stocks, mostly with Etrade, and I was a very successful trader. Commissions are the number one obstacle for small investors to succeed, and are a significant drag on even fairly large sized portfolios. For those less successful at trading, commission can put you out of business. If your gross profit and loss

(P/L) is 90,000 for the year and you pay 10,000 in

commission, you only make 80,000. If you break even for

the year, you end up -10,000. Casinos pay for their

extravagant buildings because the house always wins.

Bookies don't ride bicycles around town, they drive BMWs.

Stock brokers are no different; they are simply bookies for

stocks. I signed up for Etrade when I was a kid after seeing

their hilarious ads in the Super Bowl. What I didn't realize is

that they didn't actually pay for their gazillion dollar

advertising buys; chumps like me did by racking up

commissions. I recommend 3 brokers for investing in stocks,

depending on your situation. For small investors, I

recommend Robin Hood, which is perfect because they

charge 0 commission. Robin Hood makes it possible to get

started trading with as little as 100-200 dollars, where if you

started on Etrade with that balance, you would pay that in

commission in a year. Robin Hood is perfect if you are in

college or just getting your feet wet investing. They are a new player with a shiny App, and the best thing about them is that they are 100 percent free. For investors with a decent amount of assets, I recommend Vanguard, which also will waive commissions if you keep enough cash with them. Vanguard frowns upon active trading so don't use them if you trade a lot. Finally, for active traders, I recommend Interactive Brokers, which charges only 1 dollar per trade, and has the lowest margin rates in the business. By comparison, Etrade used to charge me 12.99 bucks a trade. As bad as Etrade's commission is, traditional stock brokers are even worse, most of them charge you 25 bucks to execute a trade, when all they have to do is answer the phone and plug your order into the computer. Don't start your trading career by bleeding tens of thousands of dollars in commission.

2. Use Limit Orders. Another rookie mistake is to rely on market orders when buying and selling. Always name your price when buying or selling. Market orders force you to take offers that make other traders (Wall Street) money every time you buy and sell. Also there is the risk that you will be taken to the cleaners when a trade is executed for a horrible price, losing you thousands. Brokers set market orders as their default setting, and you lose a little money every time they mark up shares that you buy and mark down shares that you sell. Many brokers also make markets in many large cap stocks, and will fill your order internally, meaning that they will sell the shares to you at the ask price, taking a few bucks from you, and possibly collecting a rebate from the exchange in the process for a few more bucks. Multiply this by hundreds of thousands of trades, and you have a massive wealth transfer (scam) from the retail investor to Wall Street. On the other hand, any time you use a limit order, you are adding liquidity to the market, meaning you are standing by to fill someone else's order. You are providing a service, and the bid/ask spread is your profit. Any time you are using market orders, you are taking liquidity, so you must pay a fee to do so. For day traders, the difference between getting this fee and paying it is the difference between them being profitable and losing money. Those of you who are long term investors also benefit by transacting better, making a little bit more every time you sell, and getting a little better price every time you buy. This is like negotiating when buying a house or settling an insurance claim, but instead you are negotiating with the stock market. *Life lesson– negotiating makes you richer.* When trading options, small stocks, penny stocks, or after hours, you can be taken for thousands with the click of a button if you sell using market orders. There are other benefits of using limit orders when trading. Even large cap stocks don't have a ton of liquidity at the open, so, if for example, TSLA looks like it is going to open at 282, then put in a limit order for 281, or whatever price you want. Stocks trade in large ranges in the first five to ten minutes of trade,

so sometimes you can steal the stock and turn a quick profit.

3. Avoid Penny Stocks.

Pop Quiz!

Which of the following is better to have?

A.   100 shares of a 40-dollar stock.

B.   10 shares of a 400-dollar stock.

C.   1000 shares of a 4-dollar stock.

D.   100,000 shares of a 0.04 cent stock

The answer is that they are economically the same, with

a slight catch on answer D. Beginners always fall for this one,

buying cheap stocks because they think they will get more

shares for their money. The only thing that matters is the

position value, which is 4000 dollars in every example.

However, share prices do give signals, and a share price over

15-20 is a sign of a healthy company, low teens and single

digits tend to be risky, and penny stocks tend to be money-losing machines. If you happen to own a company that is trading for pennies, you probably should sell it immediately, preferably with a limit order. Spreads on penny stocks tend to be 10-20 percent of the position value, and buyers tend to only come by every few hours or so for thinly traded stocks, so it is critical that you sell using limits. If you invest in penny stocks, you will be taken to the cleaners, plain and simple. Penny stocks are only for short-term traders, and even then, they are dicey. Remember our market mechanics equation? The equation assumes the company is making money. If a company is losing money, your earnings yield will be negative on average. Penny stocks do not make money. When Wall Street does initial public offerings for companies, they always offer them for sale from 15 a share to 20 something a share, as a way to signal that the company is healthy. There is only one way a company goes from 15 dollars to 15 cents, and that is by losing money.

Cyclical companies that aren't penny stocks lose money sometimes, but that is different. Banks sometimes lose money in recessions, oil companies can show losses when oil prices crash, etc. but their valuations go off of future earnings in those cases, and when the economy turns, they go right back to raking in the cash. Unless a penny stock company has a solid plan to make profits, they typically will burn money until they run out, and then fold. Investing in penny stocks is a scam, and odds are you aren't good enough at trading them to make money either, because a substantial portion of penny stocks are straight up frauds. The only way to win this game is to own a boiler room somewhere in Long Island or South Florida and be willing to go to court all the time against the SEC for stock fraud, or to not play. I recommend the second. As an aside, don't be fooled by looking at long term graphs of stocks that make it look like Microsoft or Apple or Berkshire Hathaway were penny stocks. *This is an illusion caused by stock splits.* No legitimate company in the United States will trade below a dollar a share. Ever.

4. Dividends are good. Even better are dividends that are periodically raised by companies that grow their earnings every year, boosting your income year after year. Learn to love dividends. If a stock has no dividend, you need to pay more attention to the company's plan to grow earnings. This is more acceptable in technology. If other established, mature companies don't pay dividends, it can be a red flag. Dividends weed out 4 out of every 5 frauds. The reason why is if the company has to find money to pay you fat dividends once a quarter, then they will have a hard time keeping paying if they are cooking the books.

5. Diversify. I touched on it earlier, but diversification is good because increases your returns and decreases your risk. We've established that the average stock market return is around 8-9 percent, but that is only the average. Of the stocks in the S&P 500, a few stocks will go down a lot, sometimes even to 0, a few stocks will decline, a few stocks will break even, most will rise about as much as the market at large, and a few will balloon, increasing hundreds of percent per year. The interesting thing about diversification, is that you actually reduce the risk of one company ruining your portfolio return, and you make sure that you get a piece of the few stocks that skyrocket. Of course, I would love to have invested all my money in Apple when the IPod first came out and made 50 times my original investment, but I would not have loved to owned a big chunk of AIG, or Citibank, or any other company that cratered. What you need to understand about diversification is that it is helpful for you, and to concentrate risk in a few positions subjects you to risk that you can't afford to take. Now, if you really believe in the next Apple, buy a few shares alongside your main investments in broad market ETFs. Investing is ultimately something that you have to own and be comfortable with, and I think if you like a company, you should take a shot, perhaps with 10-15 percent of your capital to invest. I would say to absolutely avoid having an excessive amount of your total cash in any one stock; the market can be fickle sometimes. I found that out the hard way. Diversification is also good between asset classes. Stocks and bonds tend to move opposite to each other, so when stocks have a decent sized correction, you can be in position to sail rather than swim. The more money you have, the more important diversification is. If you only have 1,000 dollars and you want to put it all on one stock, you can easily earn back the money from regular income. If you have millions of dollars in assets and your investment income is most of your income, managing risk and diversification is your most important job, because you may never be able to earn your millions back. Most people are in between these two extremes, so I think that they should try to diversify as much as possible, but I also think it is okay to put 10-15 percent of your net worth in a company that you really believe in, so long as it is a profitable company and the rest of your portfolio is diversified.

Imagine we are offering a game to players where we flip a coin. If they win, they get 90 cents. If we win, we get a dollar. We have a built in edge in this game of 5 percent (they win half the time, no edge, 10 percent edge on losses). Customers can bet as much or as little as they like. However, imagine a man in a Tom Ford suit walks in with a briefcase of 10,000 dollars in cash. He will only place this one bet, and will walk out if he wins. He wants to put it all on one coin flip. If he wins, he gets 9,000 dollars. If he loses, our hypothetical casino takes 10,000 bucks. Our average return here is 500 bucks, because he has a 50 percent chance of winning. What about the risk, though? We risk 9,000 dollars for a measly 500-dollar average win. The averages may be in our favor, but luck overwhelms any built in edge we can create. Half of the time, our man will walk out with a big smile on his face.

Now picture the same story, except the man wants to put one hundred bets for one hundred dollars each. He will likely win between 40 and 60, with an average of 50, and our average take is still 500 bucks, with much less risk. Our first line of defense against losses is diversification.

Diversification takes out the stupid, unlucky losses. Why do we care which company's hepatitis drug performs better in the market? Wouldn't we rather own a healthcare index so we win no matter whose drug doctors choose and benefit from the growth of the underlying demand. For those of us who aren't professional stock analysts, you can go crazy trying to handicap the odds. Professional stock analysts do this all day, every day, and even they get things wrong some of the time. If you have a day job, it is even harder to stay current on every factor that might affect your investments. Diversification makes it less likely that you will hit a home run, but it makes it less likely for you to strike out too. Losing money is waaaay worse than gaining it. You won't lose any sleep at night investing with a well-designed portfolio, and you can focus on what really matters in life. In fact, research shows that the pleasure people get from making money is far outweighed by the pain they feel when losing money. This is also the truest knock on using margin and options.

Trading messes with your perception. If you win, you begin to think you are smarter than you are, and if you lose, you get pissed off at the world. If you take away one thing from this book, it is that most people get rich by allowing money to work for them over time and not by anything extremely clever, at least investment wise. Professional traders, poker players and sports betters often have colossal losing streaks that threaten to destroy their livelihoods with the wrong cards or uncontrollable events. Casinos, however, are not known for losing streaks. The reason why is due to diversification and the law of large numbers.

6. Use Asset Allocation. We have established that stocks have average returns around 8-9 percent, but tend to have corrections. Bonds have average returns around 3-4 percent, but are more guaranteed. Keeping a portion of your money in safe investments like bonds that produce returns year after year helps your portfolio take advantage of volatility, rather than suffer from it. What most people don't know about stocks is that when stocks fall, market participants tend to flee to safety, pouring money into safe investments like treasury bonds and municipal bonds, increasing their values. Stocks and bonds tend to move opposite of each other. So if you own 70 percent stocks and 30 percent bonds, you tend to not have the falls that you have if you are 100 percent in stocks, and you can even outperform stocks in a choppy market. Also, you can effectively buy low and sell high by *rebalancing*. Basically how it works is when stocks fall at least 10 percent, you sell some bonds and use the money to buy stocks. Then, when the market recovers, usually about 3 months later, you have a nice profit. When stocks shoot up, you sell some stocks and put the money in bonds, effectively locking in some of your gains. By keeping the allocation to stocks and bonds constant, you can take advantage of the inevitable mean reversion that happens with stock and bond returns. The more volatile markets are, the greater the benefit of smart asset allocation and rebalancing.

7. Mutual Funds are for Suckers, Buy Index ETFs Instead.

The average fee charged by mutual funds is about 1 percent per year, which doesn't sound bad until you realize that over a 10-year period, a full 80 percent of mutual funds fail to beat the market after fees. Also, when they outperform the market, they tend to outperform by small margins, and when they underperform, they tend to underperform by large margins. The design of mutual funds forces them to pander to the lowest common denominator of investors. Everyone who panics and pulls money out of funds in a bear market forces the mutual fund to sell shares at low prices, when the manager, if he is smart, would probably like to be buying. Unlike a company like Wal-Mart, which benefits from buying in bulk, mutual funds do not receive discounts for buying stock in bulk. Running a mutual fund in today's market is like trying to maneuver an aircraft carrier on a farm pond. This means that instead of having economies of scale, mutual funds have diseconomies of scale. They also tend to be horribly tax inefficient, often turning over 100 percent or more of their portfolio each year. If they can't beat the market, why on earth do they charge so much in fees? In fact, with even limited stock picking prowess, is much easier to beat the market picking your own stocks than it is to find a manager who can do it for you after sales charges, annual fees, and commissions. Instead of investing in mutual funds, you should look to ETFs for solid returns. Investors without the time and energy to do company research all the time, or who are comfortable with the 8-9 percent stock market return over time, (I'm talking to the doctors here) should have no qualms with placing their money in any Vanguard ETF. They all come with the lowest fees in the industry, and can be traded at any time throughout the day, allowing you to set your buy or sell price at breakfast, and the order will automatically fill if the ETF reaches the price you specify at any time during the day. In fact, even highly sophisticated investors seeking bond exposure should use an ETF fund, such as the BND or the MUB to buy bonds. (Vanguard launched an ETF for municipal bonds, but it isn't big enough yet to be completely cost effective, so use the MUB (issued by iShares) to get municipal bond exposure.

8. Buy low, sell high. This is the classic response that any trader will have if you ask them how they make money, and it is true. If you sell for more than you buy for, you earn a profit; it's as easy as that. In practical terms, this means selling on up days. I only recommend selling stocks on up days. Since you most likely won't be investing in individual stocks, there is no need to panic and think that the market will go to zero or any nonsense like that. You make more money by doing the opposite of what the market is doing. Market correction of 10 percent? Excellent time to buy. When the market rallies, you cash out. Most bad investors have some element of panic when they do stock transactions. Fear and greed are not your friends when investing. Instead of panicking, do as I do. Buy on down days, especially when the market drops more than a few percent from its high, and sell on up days. Use the statistics of the market to put a little more money in your pocket.

How to Value Companies, Continued

Wall Street analysts love to talk about price to earnings multiples when analyzing stocks. The price to earnings ratio (P/E for short) is the inverse of the earnings yield. The talking heads on TV usually refer to it as a "multiple." Most first year analysts at Wall Street firms literally do nothing but analyze multiples. Wall Street analysts usually cover industries, for example, a junior analyst might be assigned to technology. So, if they take 15 prominent technology stocks, they can readily look up the earnings forecasts and, by dividing the stock price by the earnings number, figure out the multiples for the companies. By the way, most financial websites quote P/E ratios, but they are based on trailing 12 months earnings. I think this is lazy. It is the financial equivalent of looking in the rear view mirror to try to see where your car is going. Use forward multiples based on the current or next year's earnings estimates if you really want to analyze a company. Some of stocks are going to trade for higher multiples than others, and the reason why is that the companies with higher multiples usually have better growth prospects. This is also why stocks tend to spike after a good earnings report or tank after a bad one, because investors are applying the same multiple to a new, higher earnings estimate. So, if you buy Apple (AAPL), and their estimate for Fiscal Year 2016 earnings is 9 dollars a share, and they earn 10, you can expect the stock to rise by at least 1 dollar times the multiple. I am shocked that Wall Street analysts earn the amount of money that they do when usually all they do is this kind of handicapping at their desks.

To summarize, there are two ways for stock prices to rise. Either the earnings per share of the company must go up, or investors must be willing to pay more for those earnings. This is how analysts have a buy rating and 110-dollar price target of stock XYZ when it is trading for 96 dollars. The earnings for the company are 9.60 dollars per share this year, and 11 dollars next year. All else being equal, if you hold the stock, you should be able to sell for 110 in a year, based on that same multiple. However, the stock can also be undervalued based on earnings, and should really trade for 120 to be in line with the average multiple of the market. This is called multiple expansion.

Most "research" put out by Wall Street firms is really just data on the companies and some cookie cutter type analysis of this sort. If I were you, I would ignore analyst research reports on stocks, and instead think for yourself. Since analysts have are usually assigned industries, they often are given quotas for their buy, hold and sell ratings, even if their entire industry is bad. So if they are covering the landline telephone industry, and most people are getting rid of their landlines, then chances are they will have a few buy ratings out on landline companies, when what they really should say is "my industry sucks, move along and don't invest here." That is not how analysts get promoted on Wall Street. Additionally, even though there is supposed to be complete independence between the research side of a Wall Street firm and the side that provides investment-banking services to companies, this is not usually the case in practice. There are a lot of conflicts of interest with analyst's reports at large banks, and large banks put out most of the research. It is technically illegal for a firm to pump the stock of company who is giving them fees and business from investment banking, but it happens all the time. Additionally, analysts tend to be absolute sheep when it comes to putting buy and sell ratings on stocks. They put tons of buy ratings on stocks that have skyrocketed, and put sell ratings on stocks that have tanked. The Wall Street promotion machine gets behind stocks that they like, and the more people who like a stock; the more people that they get to change their minds and buy. Then, the smart money analyses the stock and how much it has gone up, decides to cash out and move money elsewhere, and the stock starts to fall. Then, because the stock has been going down a little, some analysts hop on the train and downgrade the stock, causing it to fall further. Think about it this way, if an analyst at a Wall Street firm really that good; they would have their own hedge fund. Research from hedge funds, on Wall Street, is known as "the buy side", whereas investment banks are known as "the sell side". In all honesty, everyone on Wall Street has something to sell you, so do your own work, or at least don't be mad if you don't succeed following someone else's advice.

Remember that stock returns at any given time will vary from the price to earnings/earnings yield model. The reason why lies in the statistics. Stocks have a certain variance in share prices based on supply and demand. The longer the time period, the more likely that the positive tailwinds of the company will overwhelm the short term fluctuations in stock prices. Fortunately, you don't really have to play the analyst game, we only have to understand it, and choose your investments based on your preferences, not based on the whims of the Wall Street marketing machine.

Risk Premium

There are two schools of thought when it comes to earning returns investing. The first, and most common school, is alpha. Alpha refers to the excess return over the relevant benchmark of a portfolio. For example, if the S&P 500 returned 12 percent last year and your portfolio returned 17, then you have 5 points of alpha.

Every stock manager wants to get alpha, because it means they are

competent at picking stocks and are providing value. Alpha,

however, can be hard to get consistently. Not every stock pick will

pan out. The other way to get high returns is beta. Beta is risk,

meaning that the higher return you receive is due to greater

volatility- a risk premium, so to speak. Pursuing beta can be an

effective strategy for investors, because risk can be diversified

somewhat. The most obvious example of beta is the stock market

itself- equities typically return 6-8 percent more than comparable

risk free investments. Even within the market itself, there are

opportunities to capture both alpha and beta. Over the next 20

years, I can assure you that technology stocks will produce higher

returns (9-11 percent average) than utility stocks (5-7 percent

average). The main reason why technology stocks outperform

utilities is because individually, they are more volatile, and demand

higher risk premiums, but due to higher growth, they outperform

utilities. Other ways to add beta are margin loans and options. The

main drawback to beta is that if you have the tendency to panic, you will be tested by sharp corrections, and you could lose money. The highest beta strategies typically spend 80-90 percent of the time below their all time high, but average returns are higher. I think the best approach for an investor is to keep a constant asset allocation risk model and stick to it, allowing the risk premium to build wealth, no matter the amount chosen. What you want to avoid is deciding you don't like risk and want to invest more conservative after a correction. Diversification, however, is key. You receive higher returns for taking diverse risks, which aren't perfectly correlated. That way, you can receive more return for any given level of risk, which is a win in my book.

High Growth and Momentum Stocks

There are really two schools of thought when it comes to making stock profits. Investing, which we have discussed so far, and trading, which we have not yet touched on. *Trading takes advantage of short-term fluctuations in stock prices (multiple expansion and contraction), whereas **investing** takes advantage of* *cash flows that the company makes or has the potential to make in the future.* The probabilities that the market will rise that we discussed earlier are based on the basic principles of investing, as positive cash flow is what puts gentle upward pressure on stocks. However, when you hear of people trading stocks and making money, they are doing it by predicting human behavior. You can use my model and value stocks, and over the long run, it will closely track the total return that you receive from your investments. However, the central assumption to buying undervalued stocks is that other people will eventually see what you see and bid the stock up. Sometimes good deals get even better, meaning that people continue to not see the truth about a company, and it can take multiple quarters of strong earnings to force people to change their minds. On the other hand, many of the highest-flying stocks pay no dividends, and make little to no money. This does not mean, however, that they are bad to trade. Popular stocks get even more popular as money pours in, and if you can stay ahead of the crowd, you will take their money. To succeed in trading, you need to figure out when people will change their mind on a stock and push the stock price up or down. Obviously, if you can predict human behavior ahead of time, you will make money.

The best way to make money in high-flying stocks is to ride the wave of momentum to capital gains. Keep in mind that the multiple can change too, and this will make or break growth stocks. High-flying stocks are vulnerable to *multiple contraction*, as their growth inevitably slows and the valuation of the company comes into question. What happens after is a process of metamorphosis. The company must grow into its market capitalization, as eBay and Amazon and similar stocks showed. They were beset by a period of time in which their multiples contracted and their growth slowed. This usually happens to the darling stocks. *Shareholders in such companies should ring the register when the rate of growth begins to slow, and the stock begins to consolidate lower.*

The million-dollar question here is, as an investor, what should you do with your hard earned cash? The answer for most people is that you should invest and not worry about playing poker with Wall Street by trading stocks. Playing market bubbles and high-flying stocks is fun, but remember that you only make a profit when you cash out and sell. It doesn't matter how much you go up on paper if in the end the stock tanks and takes away all your profit. No one ever went broke from cashing dividend checks, but plenty of people have gotten shit rich (or broke) from playing tech, biotech, and other crazy stocks. I'm speaking from experience, and I think the best mix is to build a solid base of cash flow by investing your money allocated for stocks and only speculate with the house's money, not yours.

Dividends vs. Buybacks

Dividends and buybacks are the two main ways a company can return cash to shareholders. Dividends are mailbox money, and buybacks turbocharge stock prices and earnings. When a company earns a profit, it has options for what to do with the cash. It can reinvest the cash in the company to scale up production, it can acquire competitors, or it can return cash to shareholders. However, companies constantly have money coming in in profits, so cash tends to build up. Therefore, most established companies return a portion of profits each year to shareholders via dividends. Moreover, many companies make it a habit to raise the dividend each year in line with growth in earnings. Dividends have the little known side effect of making it harder to companies to invest in really stupid projects because the cash has to go out every quarter to the shareholders. Dividends are usually paid quarterly to investors. Invest in a portfolio of stocks, and you will be cashing checks every month for no reason other than existing. Dividends are an excellent stream of income. Not only are they reasonably stable (companies don't cut dividends unless they are in extremely dire positions), but they also tend to grow at a minimum at the pace of inflation. Dividends also have benefits to the stock price. If a company's dividend is higher than 2 to 2.5 percent, then investors looking for yield will buy the stock if it falls to give them a higher yield. This is called yield support. Dividends are fixed and growing, so buyers usually aren't too far if a stock starts to fall.

Dividends are the most reliable way to return cash back to investors in the company. However, share buybacks are also very popular among companies. Done right, there is nothing that will juice a stock price more than a well-executed buyback. A well-done buyback can cause a stock to double and double again over the years. Lets invent a hypothetical company called Pear Computers. Pear is a stand in for AAPL, but I want to make up some numbers. Pear Computers has 1000 dollars in profit for the year, 100 shares, and trades for 100 dollars a share on the NASDAQ. Pear computers could pay a 10-dollar yearly dividend to each shareholder. Or, Pear Computers could take that cash and buy 10 shares of stock. Now, next year there is 1000 in profit again, but it only has to be split by 90 shares. Therefore, earnings per share have gone from 10 dollars per share to 11.11 per share. Therefore, Pear should trade for 111 dollars a share now.

Buybacks Traits

- Tax advantages (holders don't have to sell)

- Company can massively overpay for its own stock, destroying value.
- Can create huge gains in stock prices

Dividend Traits

- Reliable, repeatable cash
- Tax advantaged cash, but inferior to buybacks from a tax standpoint.
- Hard to screw up

Buybacks can be done right and they can be botched. Continual share buybacks at tech companies have helped make millionaires out of ordinary people. Buybacks done by big banks in the mid 2000s for 50+ dollars a share, before they were forced to the sell shares to raise capital for 5 dollars a share, made a bunch of ordinary people out of millionaires. In reality, I like to see both dividends and buybacks. They are of equal worth in my mind, and I like companies that do a little of both. I have a slight preference for dividends because they have less potential for failure, but if management of a company is halfway smart, then buybacks deliver massive gains. *If a company is undervalued, the best use of cash is to buy back stock. If the company is fairly valued, dividends are the best use of cash. If a company's stock is overvalued, the smartest thing to do is to use their stock to purchase their competitors in all-stock deals.*

REITs

Real estate is arguably a better place for cash than stocks. Commercial and residential real estate earn similar returns to stocks, but carry less risk, and greater tax benefits. Many companies based in New York from 50 years ago have since gone bust, but you can bet that the buildings they occupied are still here, and if the building was torn down, the owners were compensated for it. Even if a building burns down, any building owner with half a brain would have insurance on it so it could get rebuilt or they could receive a cash payout. The returns on real estate are the cap rate (rent divided by price of building), plus the growth of the price of the building (usually a little higher than the inflation rate). Most real estate carries returns of 4-8 percent, plus 2-3 percent growth. Also, real estate is much more easily borrowed against than stocks, and it actually makes sense to carry a mortgage on an investment property, under the right circumstances, if the cash flow from renting it covers the mortgage. Also, the IRS gives real estate owners paper write offs in the amount of 2 percent to 3.6 percent per year on the value of their buildings. That's right, the

government wants you to invest in real estate, they are even willing

to subsidize it. As far as investments go, real estate is the closest

thing to a slam-dunk that there is. Only catch is, it's really

expensive. If you don't have the hundreds of thousands to millions

of dollars you need to acquire real estate, you can still get in on the

action, through REITs. REIT stands for real estate investment trust,

and it is the term for a company that invests in real estate, and lists

its shares on the stock exchange. They are technically trusts, not

companies, but the mechanics are the same. It isn't common for

REITs to be terribly mismanaged, but some are, so the same rules of

diversification still apply. I recommend buying the VNQ, which is the

Vanguard ETF for real estate. It has returns similar to the stock

market, a nice fat dividend payout, and moves somewhat

independently of the stock market at large. I recommend 10

percent of assets be placed in this, you can do more if you want.

Book Value and Yield Support

Yield support is the tendency of investors to buy stocks with solid dividends when their prices go down, assuming the underlying business is stable. It makes stocks less volatile, putting somewhat of a floor beneath stocks that yield over 2.5-3 percent. Yield support is one of the nicer things about investing in stocks, and can help you keep your sanity in a down market. Yield support relates to the fact that investing in stocks, or REITs, is investing in the underlying enterprise that the stock represents.

Yield support went out of style in the 90s when markets traded for record PE multiples, but it is starting to come back in. From WWII to roughly 1985, the market as a whole yielded from 3-5 percent, sometimes even higher. (It yields about 2 percent at the time of writing). The reason yields are lower now is many companies prefer to buy back stock, which is neither good nor bad, it just is a change in the market since then. It also cushions the decline from a stock, as you will still be paid your dividend, even if the market falls. However the best part about yield support is that it makes stocks difficult to short. Shorts are responsible for paying the dividend of a stock that they short, as well as interest on the money they borrow. Slanting the expected return 3-5 percent per year against short sellers makes them look for easier targets. A word of caution, however, yield will not support a stock that will be forced to cut their dividend. Extremely high yields are signs of danger, as they show that the yield did not support the stock.

Another thing that helps put a floor under stocks is book value. Book value is the difference in assets and liabilities for a company, basically how much they would have left over if they cashed out and sold everything and paid off all their debts. Having lots of money in the bank tends to put a floor under a stock. For example, Apple has 200 billion dollars in cash. The company has a market cap of 600 billion dollars. Apple trades for 100 dollars a share as of the time of writing, and cash represents 35 dollars per share. Therefore, Apple will never trade below 35 dollars per share, because that is how much the company has in cold, hard cash. Book value sets a solid floor on the price of property and cash heavy companies.

One of my best investments I have ever made was Bank of America (ticker BAC), which I bought in March 2009 for 4 dollars a share. The book value of the company was 13 dollars a share, which meant that even if BAC folded, the shares would be paid off for 13 dollars. I wasn't too sophisticated yet, but that it is smart to buy stocks below book value was one of the first things I learned about investing. Sure enough, by June, the shares traded for 16 dollars, where I cashed in, making me a hefty profit.

Part 2:Investing in Debt

South Dakota has no usury laws, so dozens of credit card issuers are based there.

A brief history of the credit card

Sioux Falls is a little city in South Dakota. On the average day in January, the low is about 7 degrees Fahrenheit, and the high is a scorching 26 degrees. It is by most measures, a sleepy town with a population of about 170,000 people. Cows outnumber people. So why do dozens of credit card companies base their consumer credit operations there? And why are credit cards and other consumer credit the one of the most profitable industries in America? The answer gets back to the late 1970s and early 1980s, when interest rates were in the teens across the country. Citibank was one of the largest banks in America at the time, and like a lot other banks, they had a huge problem. The problem was the usury laws on the books in most states, originally designed to curb loan sharking. Citi was stuck paying 18+ percent on deposits, because that's what the Federal Reserve set the interest rate at the time. But, for example, in New York, the usury laws capped the interest rate they could charge at 12 percent. Borrow for 18, lend for 12, and you get stuck losing millions of dollars per day. In fact, Citibank had lost over a billion dollars in their credit card division, and they stood to lose billions more. This was so bad that it threatened to bankrupt them. They begged the legislature in New York to change the usury laws to allow them to charge a price that the market would bear, but the heavily democratic legislature was in no mood to help them. Citibank's management had to scramble to find a fix.

Credit cards did not used to be as ubiquitous as they are today, but Citibank had a grand vision for them. Adoption was slow at first, because the merchants had to have the magnetic strip reader to accept cards, and many did not adopt the technology quickly, instead relying on old school cash and checks. In that day, major banks like Chase and Bank of America treated credit cards as loss leaders, offers designed to get people in the door so they would do other business with the bank. Banks did not know how to underwrite back then, so they roughly broke even. The concept of revolving debt was genius, however. Give people what they want now, and have a legally enforceable right to have them pay you back with interest later, and you are guaranteed to turn a profit. *Interest has always been the price of making tomorrow's dreams happen today.*

This point was not lost on Citibank's senior management. And in an odd twist of history, these proud bank executives made the trip from their cushy Park Avenue office all the way to windswept South Dakota, a state that did not have a usury law, and still doesn't. Most people didn't notice, but the Supreme Court laid the groundwork for this move in Marquette vs. First Omaha Service Corporation (1978). The ruling was that if a bank is based out of a state with no usury cap, they could charge customers nationwide the rates allowed by their home state, *exporting the higher interest rates.* The only catch was that a state with no usury cap had to invite the bank to do business there. So, the proud executives of one of the largest banks in the United States had to go, hat in hand, to a little town in the middle of the prairie. They offered 400 good jobs to South Dakota in exchange for the formal paperwork allowing them to move their back office there. Citibank knew that South Dakota's economy was in the tank at the time, so they tried their best to make them an offer they would take. Bill Janklow, the governor at the time, was eager to accept the deal, which ultimately brought 3,000 solid jobs to South Dakota, with Citibank alone employing about 2 percent of Sioux Falls' population. Upon getting clearance, Citibank jacked up interest rates on New York customers from 12 percent to 30 plus percent in some cases, effective immediately. Credit cards went from a loss leader for the banks to one of the most profitable industries in history. Other states caught on to the same tricks, but to this day, most credit cards are issued out of Delaware or South Dakota. As interest rates rose on credit cards, issuers lowered minimum payments, and the American consumer couldn't get enough. Banks make tons of money off of people who carry balances every month. A lot of people just pay the minimum payments at 20+ percent interest, a factor pushing the average credit card debt of American households into five figures.

I am reluctant to even call credit cards a scam; they are almost too elegant, too brilliant to be a scam. The promise is for a better today at the expense of future earnings, at a very high rate of return for the company. High interest credit cards are a scam though, and they vacuum up paychecks. The credit card industry makes about 100 billion dollars a year in revenue, which dwarfs the roughly 35 billion dollars in gambling related revenue in the United

States. This is how the game is played, so if you want to win, you can't run up credit card debt.

You have no business investing in stocks if you are carrying a balance on your credit cards. Unless you are also in the credit card industry (in which case you would have no debt because you'd be raking in the cash), it's pretty hard to get 20-30 percent returns on your money without taking a ton of risk or being a really good trader. It has the same effect on your cash flow to pay off a credit card charging 25 percent interest as earning 25 percent in the market. Another thing is that credit card debt has to be paid with after tax money, so the interest rate on a credit card is really 30-40 percent higher than it seems, taking into account the fact that people have to pay taxes just so they can afford to pay interest on their cards. On the other hand, mortgage interest is tax deductible, meaning you get to pay for it with pre-tax money. Lesson— the government wants you to use your money to buy a house, not to get into credit card debt. There is a lot of talk by financial pundits about good debt and bad debt, with mortgages, student loans, etc.

being good and credit cards and car payments being bad, and there is a lot of truth to it. I personally think pretty much all debt is bad, and I try to avoid it whenever possible, but I also understand that if someone can earn a higher return investing than their debt charges, then they should invest until their cash exceeds the debt, and then pay it off in one chunk. However, unlike many Wall Street schemes, credit cards are actually one we can get in on.

There has been a lot of hoopla about fintech, or companies that do peer-to-peer (P2P) lending. Basically, instead of a bank lending money for credit cards and other loans, peer to peer lending companies let people loan money to their peers for interest. This is a win-win, because credit card companies have a lot of costs, such as bank branches, employees, etc. Therefore, the borrowers pay a lower rate doing P2P, and the investors earn a higher return. The P2P companies also break down 5,000 to 30,000 dollar loans into bite size 25-dollar "shares," so even the smallest of investors can get in on the action. The biggest company that does this in the US is Lending Club. There are dozens of other companies that do this sort of thing, but Lending Club is the biggest, so we are going to discuss it.

Credit cards and debt consolidation loans are extremely profitable, and until now, only the banks have been able to take advantage of this. You don't have to sit back and let Wall Street rake in all the profit, with the rise of fintech. Traditionally, if you have savings you wanted to invest, you would go and open up a savings account, which would pay 2-3 percent interest, which was safe and the FDIC would guarantee your money. If you wanted a little higher return, you might have hired a stockbroker to help you invest in stocks, or buy shares in a mutual fund. Fintech throws all this out the window. Why only let people earn 2 percent in their savings accounts, which the bank uses to fund credit card loans paying 20 percent interest, pocketing the bank an 18 percent spread on their money? There are people with cash to lend, and there are borrowers who want that cash to pay off their other debts or fund new purchases. Lending Club matches up the borrowers with investors with cash to lend, and collects the loan payments for a small fee. Unsurprisingly, Lending Club took off, and today they originate billions worth of loans every year. I think debt should be considered an equal to stock investment, and the returns on Lending Club are 10 percent plus for many investors. The best thing about Lending Club is that you can choose which loans to fund based on your own criteria. By getting in on the credit card game, you can take whatever wealth you have, and use it to compound much, much more. Prosper is the other big P2P company but I prefer Lending Club because they have a more liquid market to sell loans. All the loans on Lending Club and Prosper are for either 3 or 5 year terms, which can be refinanced by borrowers, similar to credit cards.

Tips for Investing in Lending Club

1. *It's okay to start small.* You can get started on Lending Club with as little as 100 dollars to invest, but I recommend putting in at least 2,500. You have two choices when buying loans, you can buy on the primary market, which is where Lending Club issues their new loans, or you can buy on the secondary market, where investors who want liquidity list their notes for sale. There are upsides to both, but if you are starting out I recommend the primary market, because it is easier to analyze and there are less traps, even if there is a little less opportunity. The secondary market has great deals, but it is a little more of a jungle.

2. *Don't bother buying the A rated debt.* Lending Club ranks their loans from A-G, A being the best, with interest rates around 5 percent, to G, which are dog shit loans with interest rates from 28-36 percent. F and G loans have the highest returns, and I actually prefer them to A rated loans. The reason why they are better is that everyone knows they are dog shit. The A rated loans are fragile; they come from good borrowers with good credit scores and stable jobs, but it only takes 5 percent of customers to stiff you to wipe out all your interest for the year. Since everyone knows F and G loans are dog shit (they aren't technically that bad, Lending Club won't lend to anyone with a credit score that is subprime (under 640), this weeds out bankrupt people, blatant stiffs, and most, but not all fraudsters), over 36 percent of people would have to default in any given year to make you lose money. They don't stiff as much as you would think, because Lending Club can:

1. Sue them and garnish their wages
2. Ruin their credit scores and make it impossible to borrow money in the future, effectively cutting off their access to cash

Still, about 25 percent of people who take out G rated loans end up stiffing in any given year, which is still low enough to turn a handsome profit. This isn't a saintly investment, but lending money is an effective way to achieve your financial goals. I can't say I feel bad about groups of borrowers being charged 36 percent interest when they collectively default on 25 percent of their loans. It seems unethical at first, but when you realize the stock market returns about 9 percent and this returns about 12-13 when done right, it's not a huge difference. America is run by powerful corporations who do whatever they want in the name of profit, which isn't great, but the doors are not necessarily closed on the rest of us to making money the way they do. Anybody can set up a Lending Club account; this is an equal opportunity chance to grab some profit.

3. Take Advantage of Spread of Risk and The Law of Large

Numbers People are constantly tempted to put all their money into one stock, which is a bad idea, but at least the upside potential is that if the stock becomes the next Apple, they stand to make a lot of money. This is due to the strong, positive skew in the returns of small/medium size stocks, where a few stocks end up becoming giant companies and making their shareholders 10X return on their initial investment, a few stocks tank, and most earn market returns. Loans don't work like that because the best you can do is to be paid as agreed. You know your upside up front. Your downside, on the other hand, is that you could get stiffed and the borrower doesn't make payments. Individual loans are negatively skewed investments, meaning most of the time they do well, but when they does poorly they tend to do very poorly. Therefore, you want to own a lot of loans, so any one default can't tank your account. I recommend having a bare minimum of 100 loans at 25 dollars each, hence my 2,500 dollar recommended minimum. The statistics bear this out, and over 99 percent of people who have invested in 100+

loans with Lending Club have turned a profit. Owning 1000 loans makes this even more guaranteed, pinning returns to the 9+ percent average. The Law of Large Numbers demonstrates this principle. The Law of Large Numbers states that given enough chances, the outcome of a sample will start to look increasingly like the odds of the scenario. This is why, in the end, casinos always win, well-run insurance companies always make money, and stocks of good businesses rise. You want to use these principles when investing in lending club.

4. *Use an algorithm to buy and sell.* Lending Club puts new notes up for sale 4 times per day (every 6 hours). Some notes are good deals and some notes are bad deals. Naturally, most of the algorithms that buy notes have similar inputs, so the best notes get snapped up within seconds, leaving the average investor without an algorithm to feed off the bottom. In the stock market, unless you have millions of dollars in trading capital, it is hard to take advantage of algorithms to trade, because the way commissions and exchange rebates are set up to favor the big boys. However,

marketplace lending is more democratic. LendingRobot, BlueVestment, and Nickel Steamroller (NSR) are algorithms that you can easily program to buy and sell notes based on your preferences. They are set up to do as simple or as complex of filters as you desire, and when they find a note that fits your criteria, they buy it in a fraction of a second, quicker than the time it takes you to analyze. My favorite algo of this bunch is LendingRobot, which charges 0.45 percent on assets that they manage, which is much less than a traditional financial advisor. It pays for itself, spotting opportunities based on your criteria, and can buy or sell while you sleep, steadily making you money.

5. *Eat or be eaten on the secondary market.* Lending Club is split into two markets, the primary market, where loans are offered to fund, which is where I recommend getting loans at first, and the secondary market, which is where investors sell loans to cash out. The primary market is safer, but you can get some excellent deals playing around on the secondary market. You can list your loans for sale on the secondary market for any price you want, and then

buyers can accept or pass. This is considered an auction system. The thing about markets, whether you are shopping for houses in Beverly Hills or looking to buy a lending club loan, is that what is on the market at any given time is what the buyers previously didn't want. So, if a house sits on the market for two years in Beverly Hills, you can be pretty sure it's overpriced. Similarly, most of the loans for sale on the secondary market are bad deals, because the good ones get snapped up almost immediately. However, in both cases, there is constantly new supply being fed to the market, so you have to figure out what is coming up on the market, and make quick decisions on whether the new deals are good. This is really easy to do with an algorithm on Lending Club, just set profitable parameters on yield to maturity, loan status, etc. and the algorithm will snap up any good deals it finds. If you are buying too many notes, adjust your return a little higher until you only take the best. If you aren't getting any, then lower your return until you start to get just a few, that's how you make the most profit. Also, since most investors don't understand how markets work, go ahead and list every note you own, for a high but not blatantly bad price on the secondary market (I'd do 6-7 percent markup). There is a 1 percent fee charged to sellers, so bake that in, but you should list your notes, and a few dumber buyers will snap up your notes, thinking that they are some of the better notes on the market. In fact, the good notes are snapped up in seconds, and the buyers are overpaying you.

How to Identify Bad Loans Ahead of Time

Since the maximum returns are fixed at the interest rate of the loans on Lending Club, our job as investors comes down to identifying which loans are likely to not pay back. Lending Club advertises returns of 6-8 percent, but if you can identify which notes will default, you can easily do much better. The default rate of our investments will determine whether we are successful in investing in Lending Club. Fortunately, identifying defaults is pretty easy to do.

1. Geography. For a long time in the United States, certain areas have been associated with fraud. Fraud is easy to weed out by excluding certain areas of the country that are notorious for problems. A little known fact about fraud is that South Florida is the fraud capital of the world. Whether it is Medicare fraud, loan fraud, credit card fraud, identity theft, or any number of other crimes, Florida consistently ranks near the top of the country. A combination of transience, with people coming and going from all over the world, easy access to offshore banks, and the rich-poor gap in South Florida all contribute to this problem. Fraud rates in Florida are nearly triple the national average, and over 30 percent higher than the second worst state, which is Georgia. The fraud capitals of America are, in order, Miami, Atlanta, and Las Vegas. Las Vegas makes sense because of the amount of problem gambling there (don't loan people money in Nevada either), and Atlanta is similarly known for credit card fraud, as immortalized in the rapper Desiigner's song "Panda". Desiigner raps that he has broads in Atlanta, and there's credit cards and scammers. If there are rap songs about credit card fraud in a city, it's probably a huge problem there. *Therefore, if you want to make money on Lending Club, exclude Florida, Georgia and Nevada from your buying criteria.* You can check loan statistics, and indeed, loan losses are higher in these three states. Loan money in New Hampshire or Kansas all day long, but don't touch South Florida.

2. Loan Type. What types of loans are most likely to default? The answer is business loans. Student loans are also bad, and there is a solid reason not to lend to either of these categories. The reason is that the government guarantees a lot of small business loans through the Small Business Administration, and guarantees, or outright lends money for a lot of student loans. An important rule in business is that you do not want to compete against a competitor that is getting government subsidies; it makes it very hard to win. When your competitors don't have to turn a profit, they price things too low. I believe that business owners should be able to get credit for their businesses, but the loans on lending club tend to have so many more defaults I wouldn't want to touch them. So, when selecting loan type, don't lend for education or business. Following the same line of thinking, definitely don't lend for renewable energy financing, that is an option on lending club, and it is not profitable. You would think that people borrowing money for things like weddings and vacations would have a lot of defaults, but the numbers don't show this. The obvious reason why business loans tend to default is that people get themselves into cash flow pickles by quitting their jobs, and/or trying to grow sales too fast.

3. Income- I would go ahead and set your loan parameters to exclude borrowers making less than 50k per year/4k per month. It is easier to cut back from a higher income level than it is from a lower one, and higher income borrowers have more to lose by defaulting. The average borrower on Lending Club is more affluent than you would think, most earn over 80k per year, and many have dual incomes. This also has the side effect of further reducing fraud, because most fraudsters don't report their income, although Lending Club and most banks don't verify income on every borrower, they will be weeded out some of the time. For more, check out the blog at Lending Robot, their first blog posts explaining their algorithm are honestly some of the highest level work I have ever seen on consumer lending, defaults, Lending Club, etc.

Tax Implications of Investing through Lending Club

I would be remiss if I didn't mention the tax issues with Lending Club, because they scare away a lot of investors. Fortunately, there are a couple solutions to the tax issues. At the end of the year, Lending Club sends a 1099 with the total interest income received, which the IRS expects you to pay taxes on at your base tax rate. They also send you a report of your defaults, which count as capital losses. The issue is, there is a provision in the US tax code that has been around forever to prevent tax shelters. This provision makes life hard for investors who have capital losses. Only the first 3,000 dollars of capital losses are deductible against regular income, including wages, interest, and business income. For example, if you have 100,000 invested in Lending Club, and you earned 25,000 in interest, but had 12,000 in defaults, you have a tax issue, because you are taxed on 9,000 in income that you didn't earn (taxable income is 22,000, you only actually made 13,000). Fortunately, the IRS has a way for you to have all your losses be deductible. What you need to do is to report your interest income on schedule C, and report your loan losses on schedule C also. This means, that in the eyes of the IRS, you are in the business of loaning money. By reporting on Schedule C, you now have 13,000 in business income for the year. This will also allow you to deduct the fees for your algorithm, and for other business related expenses. You will owe self-employment tax on your income in addition to regular income tax at the rate 15.3 percent for your first 110k total income, and 2.7 percent over that amount, but half of the self-employment tax is tax deductible, and you can exclude 7.65 percent of your income from it. In all, it is a money saving move, and the profits from marketplace lending justify putting up with some taxes. This issue is not exclusive to Lending Club, taxable bonds in general are taxed heavier than stocks, and all have the same interest/default taxation issue.

You can also invest in Lending Club through an IRA, which allows your money to compound tax-free, which is good also because the amount of compounding that can happen at a 10+ percent return, tax-free, is incredible. Investing through an IRA allows you to avoid paying any taxes until you make any withdrawals; at which point you simply pay tax on whatever amount you withdraw as income, and let the principal keep growing tax-free. It isn't for every investor, but I believe that Lending Club is doing to the banking industry what Uber did to the taxi industry and Airbnb is doing to hotels. They all disrupt the status quo, reducing the power of large corporations and letting individuals get a piece of the action. I recommend wading into Lending Club, rather than diving in, allocating a little money that would go into equities, and a little money that would go into bonds. 10-20 percent of total invested cash is a good number to invest in loans in my view.

Investing in Bonds

Bonds, simply put, are loans made to governments and corporations. Governments and corporations need money, but they can't really go down to their local credit union and get 100 million dollars to finance a new purchase, and commercial banks really don't have enough capital to do that anyway. So, to get their money, they go to investment banks. The investment banks take the risk of fronting the corporation the money, and then sell the bonds to anyone on Wall Street who will buy them. They earn nice fees for doing this. Bonds are a little different from stocks, because they typically trade, at a minimum, in million dollar blocks. The investment bankers typically take the bonds to a trading desk, where they are quickly sold to insurance companies, pensions, other banks, and large private investors. Most of these buyers hold onto the bonds, but some resell them, and like almost anything else, the smaller the size of the sale, the more they are marked up. A trading desk might buy a million dollar chunk of bonds and resell them to individual investors in 1,000-dollar chunks. The investors have no idea what the desk bought them for, so they get screwed.

You can't really trade bonds the way you can trade stocks, you need to have millions of dollars to play with to get a decent price. This makes it impossible for average investors to get bonds at the source. The consequence of this is that if you want to invest in bonds, you 100 percent need to invest through a low cost ETF, which buys bonds and holds them for you. This will save you a ton of money in the long run rather than trying to be sophisticated and trade bonds. You can't win trading individual bonds; the game is rigged. You can win, however, investing in bond ETFs with Vanguard. They make great bond ETFs, like the BND, which is the biggest bond ETF out there. BND owns the whole market, and is the perfect ETF for a first time bond investor. High-income investors are better off putting their cash in the MUB, which is put out by iShares (The Vanguard one isn't big enough yet). Size is important in bonds, because the biggest traders get the best deals.

The stock market and the bond market are different, but they are inextricably linked. They tend to move opposite, especially when stocks go down, high quality bonds tend to rise in price. Bonds are competition to stocks, and most investors own some of both. Bonds are safer, but have lower returns over time. Bonds, on average, have returned 5-6 percent annually. I expect bonds to return 3-3.5 percent going forward, because that's what the current interest rates support. I recommend allocating between 20 and 40 percent of your portfolio to bonds, because they make your portfolio more resilient to corrections, and give you opportunities in volatile markets. Keep an eye on the 10-year Treasury bond yield as a stock investor. If the yield goes too high, it will make stocks go down as investors rotate out of stocks into bonds. A diversified bond portfolio is much more stable than a diversified stock portfolio, and won't suffer from the same corrections that stocks do. You do, however, want to make sure that the bonds you invest in are not going to default. One of the biggest scams Wall Street ever pulled was packaging subprime mortgages into collateralized debt obligations, which is a fancy word for dog shit. Most of these were rated BBB, A, AA, even AAA, and many of these bonds caused near total losses to investors. Wall Street, on the other hand, as usual, earned commissions by the boatload off these.

Forecasting Bond Returns

Whereas stock returns come from companies earning profits and passing them to shareholders, bond returns come from owning the debt of governments and companies, who are contractually obligated to pay back your investment, plus interest. Therefore, the return of bonds can be calculated as **Interest-Defaults=Return**. Defaults depend on the kind of debt. Government bonds from the US have never defaulted. So the return on Treasuries is just the interest. On a high quality bond fund, defaults should be close to zero. In fact, less than 0.1 percent of investment grade corporate bonds default in any given year. This is partially because the agencies downgrade companies that get in trouble, and if you own an investment grade bond fund, they will sell bonds before things get too ugly. Also, when bonds default, the bondholders take over the company, meaning that the average bond default leaves investors with about 70 cents on the dollar, compared to almost nothing for the average credit card default. Defaults are fairly rare in investment grade debt, but not all debt is investment grade. BBB and higher is considered investment grade. Bonds BB and lower are considered *junk*. Junk bonds have a bad reputation on Wall Street, because they default all the time. A lot of junk bonds are for borrowers like, hotels, casinos, startup companies, third world governments, and all kinds of other borrowers who just aren't as credit worthy as big, stable US companies or municipalities. These can have interest rates anywhere from 4-5 percent all the way up to 20-30 percent. Junk bonds are a completely different animal than investment grade bonds, and some consider them to be their own asset class.

Let's go back to normal, safe bonds though. There are two ways to make money in bonds. The first way is to make money through interest payments. The second way to make money in bonds is to sell them for more than you bought them for. Bonds trade at either a premium or discount to their stated value due to market conditions, so yield to maturity is your interest rate you receive, not the coupon rate. There is an often quoted measure on bond fund descriptions, and it is called duration. Duration, in finance, is the percentage that the bond will go up if interest rates go down 1 percent (this is a fairly large amount for interest rates to move, by the way). Or, on the flip side, if interest rates rise 1 percent, the bond fund will go down by its duration. Even though bond returns are guaranteed in the long run if the issuer pays back their debt, in the meantime, prices fluctuate based on interest rates. Diversified bond funds will do fine in any interest rate environment because they are constantly either selling bonds for profit, or investing new money at higher interest rates. There is a little known force in the bond market called *roll down*, which puts upward pressure on bond prices. So, when the bond fund you invest in swaps one bond for another to keep the average maturity constant, they tend to make capital gains. Even passively managed bond funds do this automatically for you, boosting your return from 2.5-3 percent up to 3.5-4 percent per year. Bond investors make money when interest rates fall, and the prices of bonds rise, because bonds with higher interest payments become more valuable, so investors will pay a premium for them. *The way the bond funds do this for you is by sliding down the yield curve.* In a normal market, long-term interest rates are higher than short-term interest rates. This is because it is riskier to give a borrower your money for 10+ years than it is to give them your money for 1-2 years. However, if you hold a 7-year bond for 1 year, it becomes a 6-year bond. This 6-year bond, will, on average, have a lower interest rate than the 7-year bond, making you a capital gain if you sell.

Here is a snapshot of the US treasury yield curve, as of 12/20/2016.

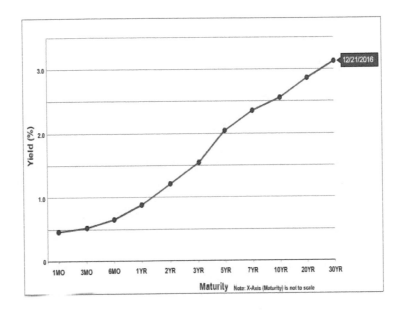

This yield curve shows you what return you can expect investing in Treasury bonds at each maturity. However, if you buy a bond, it will roll down the yield curve with time, producing capital gains. Let's assume you have a 7-year bond, and hold it for 2 years, all else being equal. When you buy, you get a 2.4 percent yield, paying you 4.8 percent on your money for holding for 2 years. Not terrible, but not great. However, the new interest rate for 5 year bonds is 2 percent, so you can sell the bond for 100 cents on the dollar, plus 0.4 percent extra for each year remaining (the market is only requiring 2 percent for 5 year bonds), which, since there are 5 years remaining, corresponds to an extra 2 percent capital gain. So, even though your yield was only 2.4 percent, you made an extra 1 percent per year by rolling down the yield curve. Bond funds are required to keep their average maturity constant, so they are constantly selling bonds and buying newer ones to replace them. This creates capital gains, which flow through to you, the investor. As long as the yield curve is upward sloping, which it almost nearly is, you will make an extra 1 percent or so per year on your bond funds. The best way to take advantage of roll down is to invest in broad market bond ETFs, or to invest in intermediate term bond ETFs. *Therefore, the return of a bond fund is Return=Interest Payments + Roll Down (Capital Gains).* This means that bond funds are more profitable than buying bonds and holding them to maturity, unless the yield curve is inverted, which is very rare.

Where to Invest on the Yield Curve

The best place to invest on the yield curve is typically the steepest part, because that is where roll down effect puts the strongest pressure on bond prices. If you are concerned about rising interest rates, you should typically invest on the shorter maturity end of the yield curve, and if you feel confident that rates will fall, you will earn the largest gains investing at the longest maturities. If you aren't completely sure, then intermediate term bonds are never a bad option. I think you can never really be too sure in the direction of interest rates, so that is what I would do if I were you.

More Asset Allocation (Why you need bonds)

Some of the smartest people I know, including myself, have at times been taken to the cleaners by the stock market. It's inevitable to sometimes not see something coming that can have a huge impact on your investments. Even though I have made good money overall, I have lost large amounts of money by missing themes occurring in the marketplace, and by stuff that no one could have seen. Who could have predicted the market fall after 9/11/2001? Markets fell 20 percent few months after 9/11, and markets were not even open for the few days after 9/11. Terrorist attacks, flash crashes, currency swings, accounting scandals and flu scares will likely all occur in any given decade. Don't think that you can see everything, and if you only invest in solid companies, you have nothing to fear. Apple, one of the best performing companies in the modern era, fell 30 percent in 2012. You can make the argument that your companies can do much better than average, and they can, but investing, like poker, relies heavily on luck in the short term. It takes a substantial amount of time for the positive returns on cash flow to overwhelm the forces of volatility. Bonds help keep you afloat in times of turmoil. In 2008, when stocks crashed, the aggregate bond index showed a +5 percent return. If you owned some bonds then and rebalanced after the crash like you were supposed to, you could take that profit from bonds and put it in stocks at historically low prices, and doubled the rebalanced portion of your investment.

How should an investor allocate assets?

I recommend an asset allocation of mostly stocks, due to their higher return potential. I personally recommend an allocation of 60-80 percent stocks, and 20-40 percent bonds. Up to 10-15 percent of the stock exposure should come in the form of real estate investment trusts (REITS). Bonds will have lower returns in the coming years due to their low yields, but they reduce risk much more than they reduce return. Investors based in the United States with over 400,000 in annual taxable income will want to substitute the bonds for municipal bonds, which are tax-free.

Sample Asset Allocation

60 percent stocks. Pick an ETF -VYM- (Vanguard Dividend Fund), or SPY (SP 500 Index)

30 percent bonds. Pick an ETF -MUB- (Municipal Bonds) or BND (Taxable Bonds)

10 percent REITs- VNQ- (Real Estate ETF)

The expected return of this portfolio is a conservative but very achievable 7.25 percent per year, which can be raised to roughly 7.5 percent by rebalancing assets each quarter. Note that there are no individual stocks in this list. Everything on this list is a low cost ETF, offering diversification at a cheap price. The only work you have to do is to select an allocation. It takes the stress out of investing, and they don't really charge much for it. None of these funds have an expense ratio over 0.25 percent per year, and most have around 0.1 percent in fees. This portfolio makes it more likely for you to have a good outcome, and less likely to have a bad outcome. Stocks, bonds, and real estate all have positive expected returns. They also have some deviation from that expected return. But combining them makes it more likely to have a better return, and less likely to have a bad return.

Part 3: Wagering/Trading

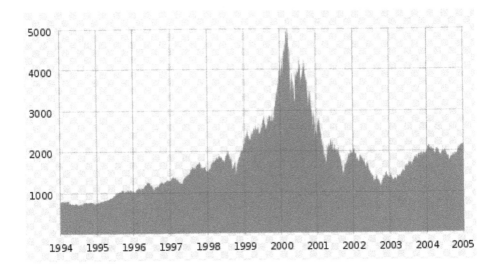

The NASDAQ Bubble, 1994-2005

Betting Strategy

It doesn't matter how much money you make trading if you lose it all in the end. You worked hard for your money, so don't give it all away with one bad decision. 2,500 years ago, the great military strategist Sun Tsu wrote that *"To secure ourselves against defeat lies in our own hands, but the opportunity of defeating the enemy is provided by the enemy himself."* You could go from nothing to a billionaire in about 6 months trading if you win every single trade.

All you have to do is lay all your available cash on the line every time, leveraged to the max. Hell, if you can win 15 NFL bets in a row, you can walk out of a Las Vegas sportsbook with a million dollars in cash. So why hasn't anyone you know made millions from NFL parlays? Going 12-3, 13-2, 14-1 will cause you to lose 100 dollars. You have to go 15-0 to win, and it's all or nothing. There's 225 different ways you can go 13-2. In fact, there's even 15 ways to go 14-1, but there's only one way to go 15-0. Laying it all on the line and hoping to get lucky is just not how you get rich trading. The way you get rich trading is to be more like the sportsbook that takes all these bets, following the advice of Sun Tsu, and letting the market beat itself. You need to trade patiently, letting each trade come to you instead of trying to make everything happen all at once. Unfortunately, there's really no good way to bet against huge long shots in the stock market in a way that would give you proper spread of risk. A famous hedge fund called Long Term Capital Management lost about 4.6 billion dollars trying to be this sportsbook in the late 1990s; they forgot to account for the fact that all their bets were correlated. In typical Wall Street fashion, they were bailed out with the help of the Federal Reserve. What you can do, however is to trade patterns that tend to repeat themselves in markets, giving you a small but sustainable edge over the competition. To make money trading, you need to understand both yourself and your competition. If you make sure that you don't lose, winning will take care of itself. Solid strategy tends to reduce the need to escalate your bet sizes also. Feeling tempted to double up and chase losses is a classic sign that what you are doing is not profitable to begin with. Casinos don't have to double up, because they design the game to make them money. The same thing applies to trading. An interesting thing is the difference in the way humans trade and the way computers trade. Computers tend to make profits on most of their trades, and to cut losses quickly, and the underlying trading strategy is the key driver in profitability. Humans, on the other hand, tend to change their betting strategy based on their results, leading to more very good outcomes sometimes, and leading to some very bad outcomes other times.

People tend to bet more when they are down, and tend to be more conservative when they are winning money trading. *To succeed in trading, you should do the opposite of this.* Let the underlying profitability of your strategies drive your returns, not luck. Trading is not about getting lucky; it is about beating your competition with a series of small edges by predicting their behavior.

The Competition

The average stock trader tends to be young, male, and have a high IQ. This is also the same psychological profile of sports gamblers and poker players. Many traders tend to be involved in all three of these activities in one way or another. Despite having high IQ, about 90 percent of traders lose money in a given year. The main reason why they lose money is due to paying too much in commission and margin interest. The shorter term the trader, the more trades they tend to make and the more they tend to lose. An average day trader with a 50,000-dollar account balance might execute 1000 trades in a year (500 buys and 500 sells, about 2 round trip trades for every day the market is open), racking up about 7,000 to 10,000 dollars per year in commission. They compete not against each other, but against specialized computers that trade stocks, hedge funds, mutual funds, and every other market participant. About 1 percent of traders consistently profit, they are the sharks, and they make millions of dollars trading, usually with the help of custom algorithms and computerized trading. In the long run, the only people who make money are the sharks, and the brokerages that facilitate all this buying and selling. How do you beat the competition? *The answer is simple; you have to be proactive rather than reactive.* Anticipate what they will do before they do it, and you have a strong, sustainable edge.

Eastern Philosophy and Trading

The *Art of War* is one of the most famous business and trading books of all time. You can apply many lessons from the *Art of War* to trading to help achieve the wealth that you want. The writer, Sun Tsu, was born in 544 B.C. in China. He was one of the greatest tacticians and military strategists of all time. The book has always been popular with traders, and was made famous by the movie *Wall Street* in the 1980s, which quotes Sun Tsu's *Art of War* throughout the script. Sun Tsu teaches us a few critical lessons about trading.

The first Sun Tsu piece of wisdom is to "Know the enemy and know yourself and in a hundred battles you will never be in peril." You are your own worst enemy when trading, 90 percent of traders are psychologically wired to panic and sell in down markets. If you fail to understand the psychology of your own mind, you cannot hope to understand the psychology of others. The market itself is your other opponent, because every other trader's goal is to make money off you. When you buy a stock, you are buying it from someone who thinks it won't go up as much as you do. If you understand how market participants are irrational and prone to panic, you begin to be able to take advantage of momentum, like in the graph at the beginning of this chapter. However, when others are panicking, you might be able to find good opportunities, but you want to wait until they will agree with you and start buying again.

There's an old saying on Wall Street that you shouldn't try to catch

a falling knife, and I believe that it is a very true saying. You don't

want to fight the market, instead you should go with the flow,

knowing how the market typically behaves and following along. Sun

Tsu says that the winning army is "like water." The winning trader is

also like water. You can't fight the market if you want to make

money. The market is always right, whether you like it or not.

Another good concept to study if you trade is Taoism, an

ancient Chinese philosophy parallels to Sun Tsu. The main principles

of Taoism are observing the world, going with the flow, and finding

balance and harmony in life. The main way that you can apply

Taoism (pronounced Dow-ism, like the stock index–odd

coincidence) to trading is to observe as much as you can without

trading. You don't learn anything from trading, in fact you pick up

bad habits from trading, i.e. if something is the wrong move and it

works, you want to do it again– confirmation bias. Another way to

apply Taoism to trading is to be patient when waiting for

opportunities. You can't fight the market and make money, so go with the flow. If people are buying tech stocks, you should be too. If the market is going down, be patient and sit in cash. The market is cyclical, like the world in Taoist philosophy, and each season has a distinct strategy. Sun Tsu agrees, "The general who wins the battle makes many calculations in his temple before the battle is fought. The general who loses makes few calculations beforehand." There is always another opportunity to trade, to make quick money. Don't rush into a trade just because it looks good. It only takes a few trades to make you rich, provided you never lose. The easiest way to never lose is to only fight (trade) when you absolutely know you have the advantage. I wish I could trade more like Sun Tsu, I tend to be prone to the same psychological flaws most people have when trading, but I've come a long way since I started. I think it is a good idea to meditate before the market opens each morning if you want to trade; it will put you in the right mindset to win.

What Trading Looks Like When Things Go Right

In my high school, we had a senior lounge. It was an administrative office at one point in the school's history, but sometime in the early 2000s, the faculty decided to give the seniors a lounge. I went to a small private school in Kansas City; my graduating class was only about 60 kids. The lounge was always just a nice chill place to hang out and study for the grades above mine at school, but when my grade took over, the lounge became known for loud music and testosterone-fueled trading sessions. We started senior year of high school pretty mellow, but things picked up quickly. I put a flat screen TV in the lounge, which the faculty did not agree with. They said if I didn't take it home they would suspend me. I called their bluff, and was "suspended" for my first day of senior year (I really did go to the principals office a lot). I spent the suspension watching a rom-com movie I don't remember the name of, and Rush Hour 2. Up to this point, I had a lot of success investing, but mixed success trading at first. I would take a step forward, then a step back. I think up to that point, I had only made a few thousand dollars from trading. I liked to play long

options by buying 1 or 2 100-share contracts, where if I played it

right, I would make a few hundred dollars.

Nick, my best friend, had other ideas about trading. His

grandparents had left him a bank account with about 20,000 dollars

in it, which he wanted to trade options with. I explained trading

options to him with the standard spiel about how if the stock went

up even 10 percent within a short period of time, he would make

fantastic amounts of money. At this point, Tesla was a very hot

stock. We liked to trade momentum, meaning if a stock went up a

lot, we figured it would continue to go up, especially if there were

significant amounts of short sellers who would be squeezed out of

the stock as it continued to surge higher.

This is a graph of TSLA in 2013 so you can see just how crazy it was.

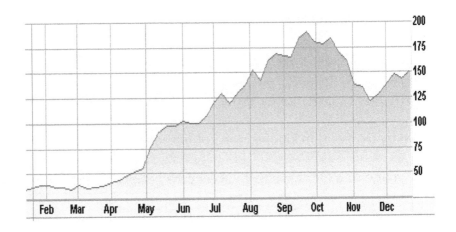

From August onward, that is exactly what happened. People who thought the stock was nonsense decided to short it, and were forced to buy it back when the stock doubled, costing them more than their original investment. This created a chain reaction, where there was little supply of the stock to buy, and desperate short sellers forced the stock ever higher, chasing the same circulating shares to ever-higher prices. The stock rose about 20 percent from August to October, and Nick cleaned up trading options. This is classic momentum trading, find a stock taking out its 52 week high, preferably with high short interest, and go long at the money call options, cashing out after every 2-3 percent move to the upside. All told, we made about 10 grand playing TSLA on the upswing. TSLA cooled off in late September, and we traded Facebook and Netflix during that quiet time in Tesla. Note that we didn't care at all that TSLA didn't make money at the time, didn't pay dividends, and was run by Dr. Evil (I'm kidding, I've got nothing but love for Elon Musk, he made us a lot of money). All we cared about is whether we could make a quick hit on it. Tesla was, and is, a long term play on the future of electric cars, but the stock changes in value nearly every second of the trading day.

Trading is about predicting the emotions and actions of other market participants over a short period of time, it is important to remember this. Whether a company like Tesla will succeed 20 years from now is not important to the success of the stock over the short term, instead, it is whether people believe that it will. Everybody loves an underdog in sports, but in the market, the cheapest stocks in terms of P/E and share price tend to look more like the 2016 Cleveland Browns type of underdog. Tesla was basically top dog, everyone loved them, and they could do no wrong.

Naturally, other kids in the school took interest in our trading, and they started bringing cash to school for Nick and I to trade options with. Being the businessmen we are, we took 25 percent of the profits, and Nick kept track of everyone's money in a notebook. That is about as blatant of an example of breaking securities regulations as you can find in a local high school. Of course, since we were young and reckless, all we did was win, withdrawing thousands of dollars in cash each week at the bank to pay back our "investors". Even the bank teller wanted to get in on our business, after he noticed all our withdrawals.

On October 2nd, a Tesla caught on fire and the stock dropped precipitously, before recovering in the next day. We guessed that if one caught on fire, another one might too. Tesla went from top dog to market pariah in the time it took to watch a GIF of a Tesla burning. From that point forward, our strategy was simple. Anytime a video of a Tesla catching fire comes out, buy puts (bet against) on the stock. Teslas kept catching on fire, and we kept making money. We made over 10,000 dollars in one 7th period Spanish class in early November, just by doing exactly that. It was a great feeling. All in all, we banked close to 40,000 dollars for one semester of yelling at computer screens in the senior lounge. I realized then that, yes, trading is a real thing, and yes, you can make a lot of money from it. We took a nice vacation in the Bahamas right after that, but Nick really needed to focus on school, so we invested the money more conservatively the next semester, picking it up later.

Trading is extremely profitable when you are right, and extremely painful when you are wrong. Trading changed my work ethic. It made me a lot less likely to want to put up with making a low hourly wage, and it made me more of a risk taker. Trading, especially if you are losing money, will negatively affect your relationships and your other work. That is the reason why I take long breaks from trading, despite making mid five figures doing it when I was in high school, it makes me very jumpy and cranky. Day trading especially makes me amped up and stressed. For that reason, 90 percent of us are better off picking ETFs, keeping commissions low and collecting passive income while growing your portfolio. However, many people want to do better than the 8-9 percent the stock market can offer. Great fortunes have been won and lost trading the market, in bear markets and bull. Most of the time when in the market, the smart investors and Wall Street firms (sharks) make a killing trading stocks, taking the money of the uniformed, the arrogant, and the clumsy (fish). To successfully trade, you need the patience of a saint and the stomach of a fighter pilot.

Trading is a Zero Sum Game

Investing in stocks yields a positive return to all participants in the market. Game theorists agree that it is a positive sum game, meaning that everyone wins, just in varying degrees. Trading is a different story entirely. It is a zero sum game. For one person to win, someone else has to lose. If you buy a stock for 100 dollars and sell it for 101.50 the next day, then the person who sold to you missed out on the gain. If you buy a stock for 100 and sell it for 95, then the person who sold it to you made 5 dollars. Therefore, if you don't want to lose money, then you have to be smarter than at least half of the market participants, by predicting their behavior ahead of time.

What compounds the problem is the commission rates charged by brokers. Commissions turn trading into a negative sum game, meaning that if you don't know what you are doing, then the more you trade, the more you lose. The game is biased in favor of the brokers (bookies) and the sharks. We are overmatched against the fancy algorithms trading at the speed of light, and the Wall Street heavyweights who can move a stock on a whim. The computers and market makers constantly hedge their positions so they take barely any risk at all. They mostly just do arbitrage and make money by trading spreads.

However, we do usually have an important advantage over the sharks and the algorithms. We are nimble. Most of us don't even have 5 million dollars in the game, meaning if we want to sell, we can in less than 10 minutes. Anyone with less than 100 million dollars in the market has this advantage, compared to mutual fund managers with billions of dollars to move around. In fact, the perfect amount of money to play the markets with is about 10-25 million dollars, because you can get preferential commissions and rebates and still be able to turn on a dime. Fund managers with billions of dollars to invest literally can't sell or buy without moving the market, and many opportunities are too small to move the needle on their assets. Make someone a million dollars who has a billion in the bank, it only counts as a 0.1 percent increase in their portfolio. We don't have to sell because some indicator that every algorithm uses goes haywire and a circuit breaker flips after they lose 100 grand. We usually don't have investors who will harass us all day if we make a bad trade or underperform the S&P 500 for the month.

You can win trading stocks, just as I have over time, but you must have the personality for it. My personality is such that I can only trade effectively for short periods and have to take breaks for months. You have to know your weakness also. My weakness is chasing stock prices as they go higher and overpaying, and cutting off trades too fast at the first sign of trouble. I also don't really enjoy trading all day, so I don't usually make a ton of trades.

If you are going to trade stocks, you are probably going to use leverage, whether it is margin or call options or whatever, but if you do, follow the advice of Sun Tsu and don't beat yourself. My weakness is cutting off trades too early, and being too leveraged makes this worse. By the way, trading stocks *is gambling*; the only thing different is the odds aren't necessarily stacked against you. Traders who don't manage their bankroll end up bankrupt. The worst thing you can do is to double up after a loss to catch up. Don't increase your trade sizes when you are losing, or you will eventually go broke no matter how good you are. This is called gamblers ruin, and it is the risk that you go bust after doubling down too many times to chase losses. I have a better formula for how much to bet and it is not the put it all on the line system (It is called the Kelly Criterion, and we will elaborate on it in a later). If you are a highly impulsive person, trading might not be for you either. This sounds silly, but you need to have a sound mind to trade. If you are in a bad mood for the day you might want to avoid trading. The market will almost always test you, and the cost of being wrong is losing money. Remember that the market will be open for the rest of your life, so you don't always need an angle, and you don't always need to trade. The deal of the decade comes along once a month, so don't beat yourself up if you don't catch a high-flying stock and miss out on major profits. With the caveats in place, what strategies actually make money trading?

Dividend Capture

Dividend capture is a low risk, conservative strategy that can put money in your pocket if you do it right. This is technical, so bear with me. Stocks that pay dividends pay them to the shareholders on the books at midnight of the record date. Because of various technicalities, it takes three days for stock to end up on record after you buy it, so the only date that matters is called the ex-dividend date. The ex-dividend date is exactly what it sounds like. Ex means without in Latin, so if you buy the stock on the morning of the ex-date, you get no dividend, even if you buy before market open. If you buy the stock at any time before the ex-dividend date, you get the dividend, even if you buy after hours. This provides an interesting trade, because dividends are usually 0.5 to 1 percent of the stock value for each dividend (paid quarterly). The stock is supposed to drop by the amount of the dividend on the ex date to reflect the lack of dividend being paid, but some stocks are more resilient, especially in the days after the ex-date. In fact, the average drop after the dividend is only about 80 percent of the dividend, which is statistically enough to profit most of the time. 75 percent of stocks recover their dividend drop within 14 days. For example, Apple pays a dividend of 47 cents with an ex-date of August 7th. Therefore, I would buy 100 shares of apple on the 6th and hope to sell a couple days later for the same or higher price. I collect 47 dollars on the dividend, and I would hope to make a hundred on the trade. *If you can consistently pocket a hundred bucks trading, you are well on your way to being rich.* You can juice your returns here with margin, also, but as always, be responsible. However, it is not as profitable to dividend capture on exceedingly high yielding stocks. Avoid short term capturing of dividends on utility stocks, some REITs, and any stock with a yield over 5 percent. These trades tend to be crowded, and in the case of utilities, unprofitable due to the large number of players entering and exiting at the same time to capture dividends. Dividend capture works best on consumer staples, oil, banks, tech, and other sectors with high earnings but moderate dividends.

Trading Earnings

Certain events can cause large changes in the price of a company's stock, such as acquisitions, earnings, announcements, etc. The most common of these events are earnings. Earnings are best because they are scheduled ahead of time. Trading stocks or their options before earnings is kind of a crapshoot, but I actually like doing it, because you have a lot of time to make preparations before hand. Sun Tsu would like trading earnings if he were alive today. The trick to making money on earnings is to do your homework. If you go to a store and the place is absolutely packed, you might guess that their earnings could top estimates. Stocks can sometimes move over 10 percent following their earnings report, so if you are right, then you stand to make some $$$. Also, it is profitable to trade stocks after events have moved the stock, if you can understand the supply and demand dynamic of the stock. Usually, the way to go about trading earnings is to make your own estimate of what you think earnings should be, and if you think the analyst consensus is too low, then buy. I wouldn't typically recommend betting against a stock because you think earnings are going to miss, you can't make as much money and you will lose more often than not. You never want to fight the tide when positive cash flow puts upward momentum on a stock.

Here's some more on my infamous Apple trade, the most profitable trade I ever made. I was a freshman at University of Miami, and I was struggling with illness most of my year there, which gave me a lot of time to do research when I couldn't get out of bed. AAPL had released the iPhone 6 in September 2014, so this earnings report was the first time the world would see how much Apple had made off the new phone. I looked at the earnings report and thought the earnings estimates were way too low. All the analysts on Wall Street were talking about how the watch wasn't going to sell, or how the iPad was dead, and so on. They were ignoring the fact that the vast majority of Apple's profits came from the iPhone, and the iPhone was selling like crazy in China and the rest of Asia. I analyzed the supply chain, and everything I saw seemed to support my thesis. Supply chain analysis, by the way, is doing research on a stock, to find out information about their suppliers. Lots of analysts do this type of research; it's not as tricky as you would think. In this case though, I felt that the analysts were all on the same wavelength, and were focusing too much on the watch, which was a small part of Apple's sales. This kind of groupthink can make a profitable trade when everyone changes their mind at the same time. I went big on this one, buying 50 contracts and then doubling down after the stock fell, buying 50 more. In all, I bought 100 contracts of Apple 115 February calls, which to this day, is the biggest trade of my life. I put up roughly 40,000 dollars to control 1.15 million in Apple stock. If I was wrong, I would lose basically all the money I had made trading. If I was right, my profit was unlimited, and I made 10,000 dollars for every dollar Apple went up. Here is a chart of Apple Stock from the release of the iPhone 6 to the month after the earnings report. (The phone was released in mid-September, the earnings report was late January where the stock fell to 110 and shot up to 120 on the same day).

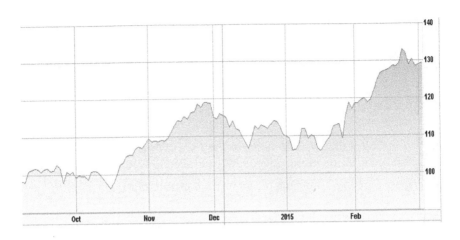

I entered the trade around the New Year, adding to the position as AAPL fell in January over nonsense rumors that the watch wasn't selling. I bled money to time premium, but the trade mostly sat still until the day before earnings. However, I was extremely confident that I was right and Wall Street was wrong. I foolishly bragged about my trade to this cute girl from New York, saying that I was going to make 100 grand that month, which, in hindsight was an incredibly dumb thing to do. At the moment I was talking up my game to her, I think my P/L for the trade was around -25,000 dollars. That's the Miami way though!

The stock bounced around in a range for most of January until the day before earnings, when it promptly tanked, sliding from 115 all the way below 110 by the time earnings were announced after hours on the 27th of January. Despite my gun slinging trading style at the time, I passed on the chance to buy more shares, and instead prayed I wouldn't lose all my profit I had ever made in the market that day. Luckily, this one worked out for me, and the stock skyrocketed 7 points after earnings, which, multiplied by 10,000 shares, put me in a good position to make bank if the stock continued to rise. My options were struck at 115– at the money when I bought some of them, and out of the money when I bought others. I enjoyed the lift up to 120, didn't panic when it fell back down to 119, and then the stock sat at 120 for a couple days. For some reason, I felt that the stock couldn't go higher than 120, which was an all-time high at the time. So I sold, and pocketed a 22,000 profit on the trade. Of course, I screwed up big time by selling out, I had 10,000 shares and the stock proceeded to rally 13 more points, costing me 130,000 dollars. I cannot even describe the feeling I felt watching Apple take off after and not buying back in, it's a feeling only someone who trades for fairly high stakes really can feel. It sucked. I got the worst flu of my life right after I sold, and didn't get out of bed for a week, and as the stock climbed higher, I wish I still had it, but worried it might drop back if I got in. I consider this trade both the biggest screw up of my life, and my most profitable trade, which it was. You can learn from my mistakes however. If you own a stock, or options in a stock that has just done really well in earnings, research suggests you should stay in.

Post Earnings Announcement Drift (PEAD) and Momentum

It is well known among market participants that stocks make large moves the trading session immediately after earnings reports. However, what is less known is that stocks that beat earnings expectations tend to continue going up. This is known to academics as post earnings announcement drift. This phenomenon was discovered long ago, and is one of the strongest arguments against markets being completely efficient. In the same vein, stocks that badly miss expectations can be good candidates to at least underperform the market. How much they go up is subject to much debate, but I would argue empirically that stocks that crush earnings expectations and deliver solid revenue and profit growth should rise by at least 10 percent in the 30-60 days after earnings. The effect tends to be most profound in small stocks, but there is still a statistically significant effect in large cap stocks. The mechanics are slightly different, however. Small stocks tend to rise after earnings because there simply may not be enough buyers to drive the price higher until word spreads and investors realize the stock is undervalued. In larger stocks, analysts are forced to raise their price targets and earnings estimates, adding more fuel to the rise. Apple after the iPhone 6 release was a classic example of PEAD.

Momentum is another strategy that produces alpha. Academic research shows that investors who buy the top 10 percent performing stocks, while shorting the bottom 10 percent of performance earn large and positive returns of 10-15 percent per year (Don't actually do this, the researchers just do that to isolate momentum from the broad market return). While I would never recommend a pure momentum trading strategy like that, the momentum effect is real in stocks, meaning that *the laws of physics don't necessarily apply to stock prices.* What goes up in markets don't necessarily have to ever go down, and often, the higher a stock goes, the higher a stock will go. Momentum is really all about feedback. People like making money, so they buy more, and people who are short are forced to cover their shorts at ever-higher prices. Momentum goes the other way though too, when a stock really starts to fall, people will sell it just because it is down, which makes it go down even more. I needed to understand momentum better in my Apple trade, if I had understood that it didn't matter if I was right and Wall Street was wrong, they had to agree with me at some point for me to turn a profit, I would have had a much larger profit. If I had waited until the panic selling the day of earnings, I would have been able to predict traders changing their minds when confronted with the numbers, instead of fighting the tide of analysts telling traders that earnings would miss because the watch wasn't selling. Momentum is less strong of a force than actual earnings data, but it is a surprisingly strong force in stock movement. I would have turned over a quarter million dollar profit had I bought AAPL options the day of earnings when the stock was in freefall. I definitely kick myself over that one, but it taught me a valuable lesson. *You shouldn't try to fight the market. Go with the flow to make money. If you must trade against the momentum, do so immediately before earnings or good news you expect, not weeks in advance.*

Trading Technicals

This is what people think of when they think of trading stocks. When using technical analysis, try to keep things simple. *Technical analysis is more of an art than a science.* There are all kinds of fancy indicators that swear a stock is going to go up or down, but most of them are revenue-producing bullshit for Wall Street. Good technical analysis relies on simple ideas– trends, support, resistance, and volume. If a stock has been going up, chances are it will continue, at least in the short term. Stocks tend to move in *trends* over the medium to short term. If a stock went down to a certain price before, and then shot up, there's a good chance a large investor thinks it's a good buy at that price, putting some *support* on the stock. If everyone is cashing out and selling when the stock reaches a certain price, that's *resistance*. Technical analysis is more of an art than a science; there are no hard and fast rules. All of these concepts are important for trading, not because they are intrinsically important, but because other traders think they are important.

Mechanics of Options-

There is no better way to juice returns than options. If a stock goes up 10 percent and you buy 10,000 dollars worth, you have made 1,000 dollars. Not bad. However, if you bought an option on the stock, you may have quadrupled your money. How is that possible? Consider this scenario. If a stock is trading for 100 dollars, what should the option to buy the stock for the next month at the current price of 100 dollars be worth? Let's say the right to buy AAPL for the next month costs 2.05 dollars per share. (Options

Contracts always are for 100 shares). If Apple rallies to 110, the same 10 percent move from above, we can exercise the option to buy AAPL for 100, and simultaneously sell for 110, pocketing 10 dollars per share. Our profit is 7.95 dollars, the 10-dollar profit minus the 2.05-dollar premium we paid for the right to this insane leverage. We have nearly quadrupled our money! Isn't that great? What's the catch?

Should AAPL fall or even fail to move higher, we lose *our entire investment.* Herein lies the rub. Options are a fantastic way to make money, but you have to be right. Being wrong can lose you money faster than you can blink. Note here what happens if AAPL goes to 100.50. The common shareholder with 100 shares has made 50 bucks. The option holder has lost 155 bucks, and he wasn't even wrong in the direction of the stock. Option values are constantly shrunk by time premium (theta). Occasionally, the implied volatility priced into an options contract will collapse, devaluing options for no reason when the stock has performed acceptably. However, if AAPL immediately rallies a dollar, the options would similarly rally.

One thing you should know is that it is always more profitable to sell the option than to exercise it. Usually you don't want to hold an option until expiration day. This is natural in the options market. Due to option values declining over time, once the stock has moved far enough, sell the options. You sell the option the same way you bought it, through your broker. Uneducated investors playing options have made a lot of money for option writers by exercising early. This doesn't fall under the category of scam, but people erroneously exercise options all the time, letting the sellers (usually Wall Street banks) pocket the remaining premium, while only having to deliver the shares for the strike price. People will make arguments about exercising to capture a dividend or because the option is deep in the money, but I have never witnessed a case where I would have been better exercising than selling. At one point, the amount of wealth transferred by people mucking this up was rumored to be about 100 million dollars per year, and there were a few traders who made an opulent living exclusively from buying the entire open interest on certain stocks and turning a profit every time someone incorrectly exercised an option.

Exercising early to capture a dividend is horrendously dumb.

Instead, sell the option, and then buy the shares at market price to

capture the dividend. You will avoid giving a couple thousand bucks

to the Wall Street casino operators. I know this happens because I

have had this happen to a couple times when I sold options, and

they gave me free money. Most sellers of options are market

makers and banks, which make steady profits dealing the spread

and writing out of the money options, hedging the risk by buying

stock. Most buyers of options are retail investors and speculators.

The further out of the money the options are, the more likely that

the buyers are retail investors.

Options Details

Options traditionally expire on the third Friday of the

month, but for heavily traded stocks; there are options for every

Friday of the month. Options are always for 100 shares, but are

quoted per share. Call options give the right to buy, put options give the right to sell. If you own an option, in practice you are always better off selling to take a profit than exercising, because you lose the time premium on expiration. The behavior of options is explained by "the greeks", which are Delta (rate of change), Gamma (acceleration of rate of change), Vega (effect of volatility), Theta (time decay of option premium, and Rho (Interest Rates and Dividends). Also, if one is to trade options, they need a working knowledge of put call parity, and the effects of interest rates and dividends on options prices, as well as a working knowledge of volatility. Strike and date selection is also imperative, and in the money options typically offer the most profit potential. A good resource to find out about all the ins and outs of options is the website Investopedia. You can spend hours there diving into the ins and outs of options markets. Options can provide you with tremendous leverage on a large stock move, often around earnings, acquisitions, and other news in the stock. Options are a commonly used tool for sophisticated and stupid traders alike.

Trading on Margin

Margin, the way it is normally offered by brokerages, is probably the biggest scam on Wall Street. It isn't inherently bad; for example, you can borrow from Interactive Brokers for about 2 percent, which isn't a terrible deal if you are a gun slinging type trader. However, at Etrade, the current rate is 9.25 percent to trade on margin, compounded monthly, I believe. We've already established that the average market return is about 9 percent, so you are basically taking all the risk to pay Etrade their interest payments, and they get all the return, risk free, automatically deducted from your account. What the hell? Why should you take all the risk, and let them set the interest rate almost exactly equal to your average profit? This is just another cleverly designed Wall Street scam.

For this reason, margin is rightly derided by the media, but is useful for traders and investors *in some circumstances*. Margin works by borrowing money against stocks to buy more stocks. You can borrow against 50 percent of your stock value to buy more stocks. If you have 50 grand in cash, you can buy 100 grand in stocks. (50 in cash buys 50 in stock, the other 50 comes from borrowing against the stock itself). Therefore, margin allows you to have 2 to 1 leverage. This compares to 20 to 50 to even 100+ times leverage gained with the right options contracts. You don't need borrow the full amount simply because you are allowed to, and I never would recommend it. A more conservative use of margin would be to have 50,000 cash paid to control 60,000-70,000 in stock.

If you are fully on margin and your stocks go down 30-50 percent, then you will be forced to put up more cash to raise the equity in the account above the required balance to carry the loan. This is done to protect your brokerage, not you. If you have a position run against you, they will call you and tell you they're going to sell your stock if you don't put in more money, both to pay the interest, and keep enough cushion to ensure they take no risk. This is called a *margin call* and it is the worst thing a trader can have happen to them. Margin is one of the reasons downside momentum exists, as traders are forced to sell their losing positions by the masters of Wall Street who make steady profits lending them money every year. Using margin goes directly against every aspect of good investing, because it forces people to sell low, and gives people more borrowing power when stocks are up, encouraging them to buy high.

With all this risk, why use margin? Margin is mostly useful for short-term trades. Margin works well, in Interactive Brokers case, when you receive more in dividends than you pay in margin interest, therefore making a profit from carrying the stock. That's why hedge funds use margin a lot, because they make money from carrying it. This is called a *carry trade*, and it is one of the most profitable things most people have never heard of, and is a favorite tool of professional traders and banks. Another reason to use margin lies in the tax deductions you receive. If you are forced to pay 2 percent on 200,000 borrowed in interest, than that can be offset by deducting the 4,000 dollars paid from income. However, the kicker is that the deduction is applied against ordinary income provided that the investor has other investment income; otherwise it is deducted from capital gains or qualified dividends (less valuable). This saves you roughly 2,000 dollars in taxes, while get you the chance to earn dividends and capital gains, which are in turn taxed at a lower rate. This is an example of tax arbitrage, and it is a pleasant side effect of borrowing money on margin. Conservative use of margin will never result in a margin call, but most investors are better off keeping things simple and staying on a cash basis.

For traders, margin loans allow a great deal of flexibility. Lets say you are fully invested, and have 250,000 dollars in the market. When you see that shares of XYZ are up 6 dollars pre-market, you can use margin to buy 30,000 of the stock, perhaps hold it for a few hours or days, and simply be debited or credited the difference made from the trade, plus dividends, minus interest. The interest is minimal, and margin gives you trading flexibility so you don't have to sell your long-term investments. On the other hand, brokerages love when people carry margin for months or years at a time, because their customers pay huge amounts of compound interest that makes the brokers tons of money.

Other uses for margin include when selling options (you are forced to put reserves in margin when selling puts/calls), short selling (same), buying stock in between settlement dates (this isn't technically margin, but brokerages consider it so), and to perhaps borrow money for lifestyle purposes, like a home equity loan.

Short Selling

Short selling, or "going short" is a technique used by sophisticated (stupid) investors to make money from a stock going down in price. It is the opposite of owning stock, or "going long". The most important thing you need to know about it is that it is mostly a scam. Wall Street, like Vegas sportsbooks, realize that people will bet more if they feel like they have choices, and normal stock ownership is too limiting for gamblers. This juices Wall Street's profits, allowing them to collect boatloads of money in margin interest, by lending out their customers stocks and forcing the short sellers to deposit collateral to cover the short positions.

Short selling is usually a bad idea, for a few reasons:

1. Asymmetrical Risk Profile- investors who go long can hopefully sell stock after a few years for double, triple, or even more than they paid for that stock if they are lucky. However, short sellers can only double their money, by selling stock and buying it back for nothing. For example, someone who shorted Lehman Brothers in 2008 would have sold, say, 300,000 dollars in stock, and bought it back worthless. This person would have made a 100% return. However, as investors in any wildly successful technology stock know, sometimes stocks go from 20 dollars a share to 200 over the course of a few years. If you sold shares in a company like that short, you would lose 10 dollars for every dollar you short. That can bankrupt you.

2. Interest. If you short a stock and it goes higher, cash will be sucked out of your account and into your brokers margin account to ensure that your broker can buy back the short position that you sold. If you run out of liquid cash, a margin debit will be created against other securities you own to, again, assure that enough margin is in the account to cover the short. If you run a margin debit, you will be charged interest, usually at 9+ percent, and it will compound. Interest compounding and an ever-increasing liability in your brokerage account can destroy your account.

3. Stocks tend to go up over time. Stocks tend to go up 8-9 percent per year. This amounts to a roughly one percent edge per month in favor of longs and against shorts. While short sellers usually look smug and smart on CNBC, it is a little known fact that investors who short sell collectively lose large amounts of money doing so.

4.Hard to borrow stocks/borrowing fees. Moderately sophisticated investors tend to ask the question, "Why can't I just short the stocks of bankrupt companies/penny stocks/inverse ETFs, etc. The answer is that you can, but typically, the higher the short interest in a stock, the harder it becomes to borrow. Stocks that have high short interest are often failing companies, and their stock will go down, but there often is no money to be made due to the high cost brokers charge to borrow the stock. This cost will also be priced into the puts, so there really isn't a workaround. Note that borrow rates can exceed 25-50 percent per year on certain highly shorted stocks, and can go even higher. This puts pressure on shorts that are in the stock, and contributes to short squeezes. High borrow rates are yet another Wall Street scam you need to be aware of.

Short selling is generally a bad idea. Sometimes, companies are simply going to go bust and money can be made shorting, but 90 percent of the time, short sellers lose. By extension, buying put options is a losing proposition unless you own the underlying stock and want to *insure* it. Puts are like concentrated short stock positions and calls are concentrated long stock positions. Therefore, calls, on average, have high, positive returns, and puts have strongly negative returns. The only time I can justify shorting a stock is what is known as a "pair trade". Pair trades are often used by sophisticated investors, such as hedge funds, to hedge out market risk from a trade. For example, a hedge fund may think that Pepsi is going to crush Coke, but is concerned about the market falling. To execute a pair trade, the hedge fund would short 1 million dollars in

Coca Cola stock, and buy 1 million in Pepsi. Pepsi and Coke are similar stocks, so a move in the market should move both stocks equally. However, if Pepsi does indeed outperform Coke, the short will lose less money than the long gains, or if the market falls, the short will make more than the long loses. The key here is to see that the positions mostly offset, hedging against a large market move in either direction. Pair trades work well during bear markets, and I recommend them as an alternative to shorting stock outright. Shorting is better done as a hedge; it is really insurance against the market going down, and insurance costs money.

Position Sizing

If you trade, you should probably keep your investment and speculation portfolios in separate accounts, due to the temptation of betting too much on one trade. A common question from new and experienced traders is how big to bet when trading. From my experience, I think 90 percent of retail traders just wing it when deciding how much to put into a trade. That, however, is not how professionals do it. I recommend sizing your trades by using the Kelly Criterion. The Kelly Criterion was invented by John Kelly, an engineer for AT&T in the 1950s and 1960s. It is used today by advantage gamblers and sharp traders to figure out how much to bet on sports, poker, card counting, etc. A few traders use it, but I think it is under used. The amount you should bet, as a percentage of your bankroll, is equal to the expected value of your trade, expressed as a percentage. If the average outcome (expected value) is positive ten percent, then bet that. Never bet more than a third of your portfolio, no matter your edge, however.

Picture this—

Let's flip a coin. If you win, you get 1.10. If you lose, you lose 1.00. Your edge is 5 percent. If you have 1000 dollars on you, Kelly dictates you should bet 50. It is mathematically proven that this increases your bankroll the fastest given any set of outcomes. Let's say you lose, and have 950. Now you should bet 5 percent of your 950, 45 bucks. This corrects for any losing streak, as eventually the law of large numbers will allow you to win, just like the casino always wins over the gamblers. The worst thing you can do when you are trading is to lose 90+ percent of your account, because it will take you years to recover, if you can recover at all. Another important thing to know about the Kelly Criterion is that even if you have a profitable strategy, poor bankroll management will cause you to lose money, no matter how good your underlying trading strategy is. There are a lot of brilliant traders who don't seem to understand this point, and they blow up their accounts, blaming bad luck. *Bad luck can't make you blow up your account, only poor decision making can.* By using the Kelly Criterion, you scale back your bets when you are on a losing streak, and ramp them up when you are winning, when you can afford to be aggressive with the house's money. Kelly is mathematically sound, by the way, and you are welcome to read his original paper, he has the proofs in it. If you read in between the lines, it seems John Kelly was a sports bettor, his paper is actually partially about bookies and telephone taps.

How much does Kelly say you should bet at roulette? Your expected value of a 100 dollar bet in roulette is -5.55 percent, so Kelly tells you to bet 0 dollars per spin. Actually, that's not exactly what Kelly says; it actually says to be the house instead, and bet against the player. Mathematics can be so simple like that, and tell the truth in a way that people won't. It is hard to judge average returns when trading stocks, and this is the main weakness to using the Kelly Criterion. I recommend using 5-10 percent of portfolio value for trades, less for options.

Where to Find Trading Ideas

My favorite place to find trading ideas is on StockTwits. They have an App and a website, which is stocktwits.com. StockTwits is like Twitter for traders, and they have a thing at the top of homepage with the most discussed stocks of the day. Most people on StockTwits are day traders. The best thing about it is that it is like being on a trading floor, people talk about all the same things on StockTwits that they do on the floor, with maybe a few more amateurs spewing their opinion on StockTwits. Most of the activity

revolves around earnings reports, highly traded low dollar stocks,

technology stocks, and biotech stocks. The best way to get ideas to

trade is to see what other people are thinking and see if you agree

with their theses. I would try to avoid most of the short ideas on

StockTwits, and I would also avoid most of the penny stocks on

there, it's better to have more margin of error if you don't want to

sell a stock you bought right away, shorts and penny stocks put you

under the gun more. Stocktwits is a great place for traders to get

ideas though.

Differences for Markets Outside the United States

Contracts for Difference–This is worth talking about if you

are going to trade London, or any other Anglo market outside the

US. If you want to trade in London specifically, you should know

that there is a 0.5 percent stamp tax when buying shares in London.

You should also know that the stamp tax makes it nearly impossible

to trade. So, instead of shares, CFDs are used in London, because there is no stamp tax. CFDs are basically when the broker is the bookie, and the trader is the bettor. They are a bet on the direction of the stock, and if the stock goes up, the broker pays you the difference in the stock; multiplied by the number of shares you did your contract for on your order. CFDs are like stocks on steroids. Stockbrokers being the bookies they are, they let people bet on credit, so if you have 1000 dollars, they might let you bet on 10,000 worth of stock, so if the stock goes up 10 percent, you would make 1,000 on your 1,000 dollar investment. If the stock goes down 10 percent, they will hit you with a margin call—easy come, easy go. An interesting thing about CFDs is that they receive dividends just like stockholders, but they also charge interest on the borrowed money in the contract. The CFD is most common in London, but they also exist in other markets, such as Australia, Canada, Japan, and most of the Eurozone. They are actually *illegal* in the United States. So are CFDs just too good for the United States to handle? Maybe, but they tend to get people in trouble who aren't responsible with leverage.

Where to Trade Outside The United States

I recommend investing in the following markets- London, Singapore, Australia, the United States, and Hong Kong. They all are English speaking, and only the US imposes any tax whatsoever on foreigners trading, which is a withholding tax on dividends, and they withhold 15 percent, typically. Feel free to invest in any market that you choose, but know that these are the most stable markets. For those who want to exposure to China, the best way is to do so through Hong Kong and Singapore. They combine explosive Asian growth with the comfort of the Western legal system. Australia, Canada, New Zealand, and the US also are all stable countries with good opportunities to invest. Investors will automatically get currency exposure when they invest in any given market, but it is always good to get US dollar dividends, which are common in the UK and Australia. If you prefer other markets, like Latin America, Europe or other parts of Asia, feel free to pursue them, but understand that not all countries enforce common sense rules to prevent blatant stock fraud the way the US and UK do.

Foreign market quirks

As opposed to the United States, in foreign markets, it is not uncommon for stocks to trade for low values. This is not as much of a signal of poor financial health as it would be in the US. In London, shares are often quoted in pence. Stamp taxes on buys and sales (usually 0.5 percent or so) are often imposed, so check the rules before you buy. Lastly, invest in what you can understand. This especially applies to China, but avoid companies with little disclosure, and no reports in English. This is just common sense, Chinese stocks are better than penny stocks, but there is a lot of stock fraud in China, it often isn't regulated the way western markets are.

Part 4: Taxes on Investing and Trading

Investors in the United States are responsible for paying taxes on their trading profits. Taxes are no fun to pay, but they are an expense that can be reduced if you take advantage of the sections of the Internal Revenue Code meant to benefit you. Here are the Federal Income Tax Rates for 2016.

Rate	Single Filers	Married Joint Filers	Head of Household Filers
10%	$0 to $9,275	$0 to $18,550	$0 to $13,250
15%	$9,275 to $37,650	$18,550 to $75,300	$13,250 to $50,400
25%	$37,650 to $91,150	$75,300 to $151,900	$50,400 to $130,150
28%	$91,150 to $190,150	$151,900 to $231,450	$130,150 to $210,800
33%	$190,150 to $413,350	$231,450 to $413,350	$210,800 to $413,350
35%	$413,350 to $415,050	$413,350 to $466,950	$413,350 to $441,000
39.6%	$415,050+	$466,950+	$441,000+

The rates are graduated; meaning the portion of your income over certain thresholds is taxed higher than the first few dollars of income. The main thing that the government does to encourage long-term investment is to allow a lower rate of tax for long-term capital gains, which are gains on securities held more than one year, and for dividends. Look at the chart above; if your rate is 10-15 percent for taxable income, your capital gains/dividend rate is 0. If you are under the top tax bracket, your rate is only 15 percent, and if you are in the top bracket, your rate is 20 percent. Also, people who make over 250,000 per year have to pay 3.8 percent for the Obamacare surtax, but Trump and the republican congress should repeal that tax so it shouldn't be an issue any more. Taxes could be higher on stock and bond investments, but the situation isn't ideal. However, there are a multitude of strategies you can use to cut your taxes, no matter your situation.

Tax Saving Strategies

Legally speaking, you can use a variety of tax shelters to save money. These strategies are all legal, require varying investments and generate write offs or exemptions from tax. However, also included is some smart business planning to save taxes, such as splitting income, using S Corps and LLCs to save payroll taxes, and estate tax saving/asset protection moves. Even for those of us without Swiss bank accounts, there is hope to pay less tax. Here are a few examples of ways you can defer, reduce or avoid tax.

Municipal Bonds

Investment grade municipal bonds are roughly as safe as treasuries, and earn higher returns, tax-free. Interest from municipal bonds (munis for short) is 100 percent tax-free at the federal level, and if munis are in state, they are tax-free at the state level too. (New York, New Jersey and California residents in particular may want to consider finding ways to invest in their own state's municipal bonds, if they trust their states not to go broke) Average muni returns are 4-5 percent in the long run. Municipal bonds might yield 3 percent, and at a 40 percent tax rate, this is equivalent to earning 5 percent in a regular bond. They are a much better deal for high-income investors. *The weighted average tax rate of market participants is about 15 percent. This means that the prices are set for stocks, bonds, etc., assuming a 15 percent tax rate.* This is because there are large groups of investors that pay no taxes on their investment gains, including foreign businesses, governments, domestic pension funds, and all retirement accounts. Roughly 50 percent of total market participants don't have to pay capital gains tax or tax on bond interest. However, if you are investing in a taxable account, you do. Therefore, if you are in a high tax bracket, putting municipal bonds in your taxable accounts to take advantage of tax free interest is simply a no brainer.

Individual Retirement Accounts (IRAs) and 401(k) Accounts

Even though stock profits are taxed as ordinary income if they don't qualify as long-term capital gains, the government still wants you to invest and build your savings. They particularly want to you save money to fund your retirement, which is why they allow you to deduct 5,500 a year (6500 if you are over 50) from your taxes when you contribute to an IRA. Then, the money is allowed to grow tax-free until you need it. You can begin taking withdrawals without penalty over the age of 59 ½. There are some complicated rules around the tax benefits of IRAs, but they typically allow you to defer income to later years. Even better is the fact that you can make contributions for the last year as long as you do it before April 15, and get a tax refund for contributing money. Self employed individuals get even more benefits, and can set up self employed SEP IRAs, which have higher contribution limits (53k per year, subject to limitations). If you have extra money and want to defer taxes, these are a great way.

If your IRA gets really big, perhaps due to making smart investments, or from funding it the maximum amount for years on end, you can tap your IRA using what are known as SEPP payments. SEPP stands for substantially equal periodic payments, and there are different ways to calculate it, but the gist of SEPP payments is that you can take them at any age; you don't have to wait until 59 ½ to take them. This means that IRAs don't necessarily have to be used for retirement, only for long term investing, and your money is not as frozen as it seems.

Employer sponsored 401(k) plans are also a good option, but they are less flexible. The best part about 401(k) is that employers usually will do a 50 percent match on your contributions up to a certain amount; some generous companies even do 100 percent.

401(k) accounts have contribution limits of 18,000 per year (24,000 if over 50). I always recommend rolling them over into an IRA, to take control of the accounts from your employer, especially if you change jobs. IRAs, SEP IRAs and 401(k) accounts are excellent ways to defer taxes, and deserve a place in your portfolio.

Real Estate

Real estate offers tax advantages, steady income, and leverage. I love this example, so I'll use it again. How many companies from 100 years ago are still around? Not many. How many buildings built 100 years ago are still here? Most, especially considering that even if the building is torn down, they still have to pay the owner for it. Tax benefits of real estate:

- Depreciation- improvements (anything but land) on residential property can be depreciated over 27.5 years and commercial property over 39 years. Additionally, cost segregation on high value properties increases this write off by 30-40 percent per year.

- Leverage- 20 percent down is typical for real estate, which means that investors get 5 times leverage. If you buy a 500,000-dollar property with 100,000 down, and it appreciates 20 percent, you have doubled your money. Investors don't *need* to take advantage of leverage, but they can. Also, note that the depreciation would be 2-3 percent of the 500,000, not the 100,000.

- Deferral- 1031 exchanges eliminate capital gains on the exchange of real property. Investors can also do an installment sale when they sell the property to defer taxes and earn interest.

- Rent- Most properties rent for 5-8 percent of their market value each year, and rents rise over time. This can be a higher return than the stock market.

Real Estate Example:

Property value- 1,000,000

Down Payment 350,000

Loan 650,000 at 4.5%

Rent +100,000 per year

Expenses -25,000 per year

Property Taxes -10,000 per year

Interest -29,250 per year

Cash Flow=35,750 per year

Depreciation (only on paper) -35,000 per year.

Taxable income=750 dollars per year

In this case, 35,750 dollars in income became less than 1,000 on paper, 100 percent legally. This can even create paper losses sometimes, and even though they are typically limited by the IRS passive activity loss rules, meaning they can't offset your income from your job or business, they can definitely offset rent from other real estate.

Oil Investments

This one is the big kahuna. Many members of congress remember the oil shocks of the 1970s, and do not want to ever go back to that situation. They allowed US oil to become the anointed industry as far as taxes are concerned. What readers should know is that the US tax code used to be chock full of loopholes that wealthy people could use to avoid income and estate taxes. Even though the top rate the 1950s was 90 percent, most high-income earners paid less than 15 percent. The reason why is because they used tax shelters and loopholes to pay no taxes, often showing losses when they were raking in the cash. They used real estate limited partnerships, oil investments, muni bonds, fancy financing arrangements, agricultural ventures, equipment leasing, motion picture investments, and of course, offshore tax havens to pay virtually no taxes (All of theses shelters are still around in one form or another, but some have been pared back by the passive loss rules). When the 1980s rolled around, Reagan was popularly viewed as a hero for cutting taxes from ridiculous rates to reasonable ones.

What people don't realize is that he didn't actually cut taxes; he just made the code simpler. However, the oil shelter stayed.

Here is how it works—There is a shelter called the ODDS shelter. It stands for oilwell drilling deduction system. This shelter is unique in that it reduces your Adjusted Gross Income (AGI), which can have some interesting and unintended consequences, since AGI is what most phase-outs and tax credits are based on. Whether you take advantage of that or not is up to you, but it was designed by congress to subvert the typical tax system. This shelter gives tax write offs of 90 cents for each dollar invested in the first year. It involves drilling oilwells for a working interest, and within 7 years, investors should get 2 dollars in tax savings for every dollar they invest. Additionally, the returns from investing in oil are high on average. To maximize the tax benefits, and reduce the odds of drilling a dry hole, you should invest in only developmental wells, which are different from wildcat wells. Developmental wells are proven wells in existing oilfields. They lack the explosive upside potential, but 95-98 percent of them succeed.

By having the investment pay for itself in tax benefits, the expected value of the investment is skewed in your favor, much like the casino at the blackjack table. While it is possible to lose money, the geometric mean outcome is skewed to the positive side by hundreds of thousands to millions of dollars. The odds are stacked in the favor of the investor, because the US government is subsidizing oil to reduce our dependence on third world dictators and OPEC. In the worst-case scenario, on a 500,000-dollar investment, you write off the entire investment. If you would have not made the investment, you would have had to pay 250,000 in taxes, so you only lost 250,000 dollars net. If the oilwell produces, you receive income that is 30-40 percent free of tax, and you did not have to pay taxes on the initial investment. This is what is known as a deferral and conversion shelter. Oil is known for its ability to make people rich, so if the 500,000 dollar well strikes big oil, you now have 100,000 to 200,000 dollars a year in income for life, 40 percent exempt from tax.

Oilwells are considered real property (real estate), consisting of land and appurtenances. The courts agree with this distinction. Therefore, under the definition of section 1031, it is possible to exchange oilwells for any amount real property of your choice with favorable tax implications.

The tax deductions come off the highest bracket in your income, saving you more money than your average tax rate would suggest, since the tax code is progressive. The only limitation is that the Alternative Minimum Tax (AMT) can defer deductions if you make investments exceeding 40-50 percent of your income for the year. The money you use to invest can come from savings, but deductions come off your highest dollar of income. This shelter is ideal for athletes, entertainers, lottery winners, and other temporary high earners who want to defer income and avoid paying tax.

The deductions come from Intangible Drilling Cost (IDC), Bonus Depreciation, Depletion Allowance, and Section 179 and 199 deductions.

Example:

Invest 1 million dollars in oilwells out of AGI of 1.5 million for 2014

900,000 dollar write off first year (800,000 IDC deduction, 100,000 depreciation)

300,000 dollar gross income first year, 200,000 net

45,000 dollars in depletion

155,000 net income

10,000 dollar section 199 deduction

145,000 taxable income-900,000 dollar write off.

Cash flow= +200000 for year. Taxable income=-700,000 from project.

Investing in oil is extremely complicated, so you definitely need the advice of CPAs and people who specialize in oil and gas. Oil and gas also requires substantial investments, like over 250,000 dollars per investment, so it is not ideal for everyone, but it is a neat tax shelter and has high economic returns.

Income Splitting

Own a business, and want to reduce your taxes? Put your kids on payroll. Anyone who has a lower tax rate them you, you can pay wages, and write off the money you pay them. In effect, you are moving income from your tax return to theirs, if they even need to file one. (Less than 10k in income and you usually don't have to file). Also, you can have everyone work for you and help your company. Also, you can set up brokerage accounts in your kids' names, and invest for their futures. The so called "kiddie tax" limits this benefit on investment income to 2,000 dollars a year, but it is still effective for some clients. Income splitting has been pared back a lot in the last 50 years, but you do get a slight benefit from splitting income between corporations and trusts, which all have their own social security numbers, and tax brackets.

Payroll Tax Planning

Incorporate your business as an LLC or an S Corp. If you don't have one, then make one. Instead of reporting income on income on Schedule C, you pay yourself a wage and dividends. The wages will have regular payroll taxes, but the dividends are payroll tax-free. You need to pay yourself a "reasonable wage" 30 to 50 thousand dollars per year or a third of your income, whichever is less. There is a lot of litigation over this between the IRS and people that don't pay themselves any wage at all, but properly used, this is a legitimate strategy that helps keep total tax expense low. Dividends from a business you participate in are not subject to self-employment tax or the 3.8 percent Obamacare surtax. Paying less taxes is only half the battle, you also want to make sure you protect your assets from any potential threat.

Asset Protection

The Four Threats to Wealth

There are four things that will destroy your wealth. They are:

1. Divorce. While most people don't get sued for millions in their lifetime, half of marriages end in divorce, and when there is money to fight over, fights happen. Depending on what state you live in, you can lose half your assets in divorce. There's an old saying that you can't get blood from a turnip, but if you have money, you are not a turnip.

Cutting edge asset protection renders prenups obsolete, replacing it with stronger protection, protection that you don't need to force anyone to sign anything for.

2. Taxes. The IRS has broad powers to sue you to collect tax, and can levy wages and bank accounts. The IRS is about the worst creditor you can go against, so don't stiff them, instead work with the tax code to reduce your taxes in legitimate ways.

3. Estate Tax. While it is likely to be repealed, losing 40 percent of your wealth with each generational transfer will destroy wealth if given enough time.

4. Lawsuits. If you live in the wrong state, are a doctor, or own a business, then it is possible to lose all your money to a lawsuit. Use proper asset protection, and potential plaintiffs can forget about getting about taking your money.

Wealth- Then and Now

To fully understand wealth today, one must first understand wealth in history. Going back to ancient times, wealth has rested on ownership of land. In Ancient Rome, families became enormously wealthy by the ownership of huge estates and apartment buildings. They would make their money by renting the apartments to tenants and leasing farmland for a cut of the profit. The roman aristocracy, however, eventually met its end when the barbarians burned their houses and carried away their worldly possessions. However, before long, all over Europe, families began to accumulate land. They lorded over their land, collecting rent and becoming very wealthy. From this point on, wealth was rarely destroyed, only spread out among more and more descendants. The wisest of the families limited the number of children they had to 2, maybe three children, who in turn married well. Therefore, the fortune would not be diluted amongst more and more descendants. In England, Spain, Portugal, Italy, Germany, and the rest of Europe, the aristocracy found themselves in possession of large quantities of land, which they have used to cement their status to this day.

However, as time went on, merchants and moneylenders became increasingly rich from finance. They joined the upper classes too with their ballooning fortunes. The point here is that there are thousands, maybe more people in Europe and the United States who do not need to work, because they are covered by dynasty trust funds and the income they provide. However, they had to do this a specific way, and a few inept aristocrats were faced with some new problems, other than the usual gambling problems or overpopulation of families.

Until World War One, there were usually no or low inheritance taxes to be paid, so wealth could build up, generation after generation. The onset of inheritance taxes, in Britain and the US, in particular, devastated families who weren't adept at the use of trusts and offshore structures. Some countries were more generous; Portugal, for example, never imposed an inheritance tax. Taxes could be imposed at rates up to 70 of total assets percent upon death. Therefore, the families who did not hide their wealth from the state found that they were suddenly impoverished, ruining all of their ancestor's prudence and preservation. Most of Europe changed their tune just 40 years later, and after 1975, the only Anglo country to tax ownership of farmland on death was and still is the United States. However, the aristocracy tended to run in the same circles, so wealth disappeared into thousands of trusts, or was carried, *suitcase by suitcase*, to Switzerland, to Monaco, or other tax havens. Therefore, the amount of wealth held away from the clutches of the tax authorities in Europe grew exponentially, while those held by those too stupid or lazy to move it ended up in the government coffers. American's who had always been more new-money than their European counterparts, tended to rely more on fancy estate planning techniques to cut their estate taxes, or simply paid them.

What can those of us who aren't aristocrats learn from aristocracy? First, think in terms of being a steward of our wealth. If you have a substantial investment portfolio, it is yours for the rest of your life, and after that, it will be your heirs. Therefore, you should only use the *income* from your wealth for our lifestyle, leaving the *principal* as a fortress that will grow faster than inflation, generating even more income over time. Your goal should be to have enough income from wealth to support you and your family without having to ever work again.

Secondly, place assets in trusts. Governments have a long track record of redistributing wealth from one group of citizens to another, and even though America isn't like that for the most part, being on the wrong end of a lawsuit can result in all your money being taken from you. If a landed family in the old days were not prudent enough to transfer wealth where it wouldn't be heavily taxed, they would have eventually found themselves with no money. You never want to do anything to decrease your family's wealth in the long run. This includes selling assets and taking loans out to fund lifestyle, rather than relying on interest, rent, dividends, and gains. This also includes being careless about marriage and divorce. Also, gambling is something that should not be done with any more than your monthly income, as many aristocrats have proven. Families who have stayed wealthy have done so because they have protected their assets from bad investments, from their governments, and from themselves. Trusts are necessary for this purpose, to protect you from others, and sometimes from yourself. The art of protecting assets is something that every financially successful person needs to learn.

What is Asset Protection?

Asset protection is putting assets where they cannot be taken from you. I recommend use LLCs, asset protection trusts, and sometime even offshore structures to protect assets. Properly done, it is impenetrable. This part of the book is concerned mostly with protecting assets, not saving taxes. This area is the area that most professionals and other high earners are particularly ignorant of. How to properly structure a business simply is not taught in school.

Limited Liability Companies

When doing business, 99 percent of the time, the correct way to incorporate will be to form a Limited Liability Company (LLC). A Limited Liability Company is exactly what it sounds like- it limits the liability from the company. LLCs provide protection for your personal assets against business debts (outside protection), and protection for assets inside the business from your personal debts (inside protection). For example, outside protection means that if your business borrows a million dollars to buy equipment and fill orders, and business goes south in a bad economy, then the bank can take all the equipment and sack the company, but they cannot, for example, sue to take away the person's personal bank accounts. You are also going to want to avoid ever signing a personal guarantee on a loan, as it will invalidate all your asset protection you gain from having an LLC. There are two kinds of asset protection, protection from inside liability, and protection from outside liability. Inside liability protection means that the company cannot be taken over to pay its owner's personal debts. This is unique to LLCs. While regular corporations provide outside protection, meaning that you cannot be pursued personally to pay business debts, only LLCs can offer your business protection against your personal debts. Another feature of LLCs is pass-through taxation, which means that company's profits are not double taxed. C corporation profits are always double taxed. Not all states are equally friendly toward LLCs, so it is important to incorporate in a friendly state, such as Nevada, Delaware, or New Mexico. This can be done cheaply online. LLCs can be combined with asset protection trusts if maximum protection is desired. Different states LLCs are useful for different purposes. Nevada is a great state for most purposes regarding asset protection. New Mexico LLCs are ideal as a stand in when buying property, such as vehicles or real estate. There are actually no disclosure requirements for New Mexico LLCs. They allow you to anonymously own things, which is a huge benefit in asset protection. What cannot be found cannot be stolen. You can also pay bills and set up credit cards in the name of these LLCs. It is a virtual requirement for asset protection that things be owned not in your own name but in the name of an entity you create. As

John D. Rockefeller once said you want to *own nothing, but control everything.* Legal title offers nothing to the person who owns it. Legal title only allows the government to tax you and take things from you. What is more important, title to a car, or the keys? The keys are all you need to enjoy the car, so let your LLC own things, and simply enjoy them. A friend of mine who's father owns a good deal of property once told me that nothing was in his name-except for the bills. All the assets were held in other people's names, in trust, or in a corporation, but the bills all went to him. This is a solid use of asset protection.

How to Move Assets for Asset Protection

Chances are if you have any wealth at all, you own some things in your own name. That is okay, but if you want to protect your assets from potential creditors, like people you might bump into on the freeway, or who spill coffee on themselves in your business, you need to move the assets out of your name.

Real estate is quite easy to transfer. All you need to do is file a quitclaim deed with the county granting your ownership interest to a LLC or Trust you have set up. You may want to have your lawyer help you with this, or you can do it yourself. This way, if you are sued by someone and they win, for example, they can take your property, but the house is no longer your property because you gave it away. (Note that if you have a mortgage on the property, you are still liable for the mortgage).

I'm sure some of you are thinking that's crazy talk, and that you can't just steal things and give them away to prevent them from being taken back, and you are mostly right. There is a mechanism for invalidating such transfers, and it is called the Uniform Fraudulent Transfer Act. You cannot give things away once there is a judgment against you, or even if there is one about to be dropped on you, in the hope that you won't be discovered. However, doing so before you get into trouble will bar creditors from collecting. Cars can be similarly retitled, and you may or may not find it necessary to do so. You probably will want to if you have multiple cars, expensive cars, or antique cars. At the very least, you could start buying your new cars in the name of your New Mexico LLC or other similar entity.

Bank accounts present an interesting case. Creditors can often levy bank accounts of yours if they get a judgment against you, and certain creditors, like the IRS, don't even need to go to court. You might want to consider taking out a bunch of cash from the bank, and putting it in a safe deposit box at another bank, or getting a good safe for your house, because creditors cannot levy cash. This is legal, but banks frown upon having large amounts of cash in their vaults, for insurance purposes. Tell them you want to store legal documents; they won't question a word of it. By the way, an interesting historical tidbit is that the IRS allows you to deduct safe deposit box fees as miscellaneous itemized deductions, and has for a long time, as long as you tell them what bank the box is at. There is no social benefit to bank box fees being tax deductible. Could it be that when they put in into law they wanted to know where people kept their cash? In any case, the IRS isn't a creditor I would want to square up with in court, but if you don't want them to know where you keep your box, don't try to write it off on your tax return. From an asset protection standpoint, the more you use cash, the better. Cash is king.

Estate Planning

Estate planning is a phrase that is tossed around often among wealthy families. It means arranging a few things so you don't have to pay as much transfer taxes upon death. The estate tax is deeply unpopular, and is likely to be repealed by the Trump Administration. If they repeal the tax by the time you're reading this, just skim it, you won't have to read it too closely. The simplest and most effective way to "estate plan," is to spend your money down to the exemption. Currently, in the United States, the first 11 million dollars of a couple's wealth are not subject to estate tax. The amount over that is subject to estate tax. Therefore, if you have 12 million in assets, you may want to consider spending some or giving some away (you can give 28,000 per year to as many people as you like without using any of your 11 million dollar exemption).

The first step to beating the estate tax is understanding it. Very few estates are now required to file returns–less than half of a percent. Therefore, the expectation is not for an estate to owe tax, but for an estate to not owe tax. It could therefore be somewhat difficult for the IRS to know what you own, and they tend to audit extremely wealthy people to try to figure out how much they make. Assuming the estate is larger than the 11 million dollar threshold that currently must pay tax, what is part of the estate? The answer is that all the property held in the name of the deceased, like stocks, bank accounts, and real estate, as well as anything given away in the last three years.

The three-year rule provides an interesting in between the lines way of looking at the estate tax. If something was given away prior to three years of death, then it probably won't make it on the return. If the IRS audits an estate and tries to find assets, they can go back six years. They have no power to go back further than 6 years for the most part. This is also true for income tax purposes. That means that people get away with doing aggressive tax shelters all the time, because the IRS only has so much manpower. Property ownership is quite opaque if the beneficiary of the property does not own the property. It gets nearly impossible to unwind if you throw offshore bank accounts and trusts into the mix. The Achilles heel of the estate tax is noncompliance and aggressive planning. There is constant litigation surrounding estate tax returns, since families involved are often some of the most powerful members of society. It is really a waste of energy on both sides of the equation. The IRS collects roughly 80 percent of the income tax they are due, ranging from about 99+ percent on wages withheld, to about 50-60 percent of taxes that small businesses pay. The noncompliance rate on the estate tax is most likely around 50 percent, due to the logistical nightmare of finding out where all the assets are.

Where they have succeeded most in collecting tax, unfortunately, is with people with businesses and farms that they want to pass to their children, especially when the owners die young. Setting up family limited partnerships and other estate planning techniques cuts the effective level of tax to around 15-20 percent on the value over the 11-million dollar exemption. Recognizing this, congress enacted a few provisions meant to protect small business and farms from the estate tax, but they don't provide enough relief.

The classic way to avoid estate taxes used by business owners in the 50s and 60s was called a preferred stock recapitalization. It worked by exchanging the owner's common stock for preferred stock, which would pay dividends for life. The common stock then has a low fair market value, perhaps 80 percent lower, and can be given to the kids. Also, any future appreciation and earnings growth accrued to the common stock that was given to the kids. This is called an estate freeze, and it moves future appreciation out of the wealthy person's estate. All in all, it reduced estate tax from 70 percent to about 10 percent. Estate freezes are still alive and well, and should be used any time assets are appreciating in value, if the owner of the assets chooses the domestic route of planning. The best way to reduce the estate tax has three steps:

- 1.Freeze the value of the estate
- 2.Use valuation discounts when gifting
- 3.Use cash from your estate to pay expenses for trust, especially taxes

These can be combined in what is known as an "intentionally defective grantor trust". It works as assets are sold to a trust owned by the children of the grantor (person with the money). The grantor sells them the business, and they pay him back with interest at a later date, freezing the value of the business or other assets. The grantor's estate will increase by the low interest rate he receives, not the appreciation in business value.

Historically, about a third of the value of companies and real estate escaped estate tax due to the owners undervaluing of assets compared to what IRS would have liked. Value is in the eye of the beholder, and the IRS cannot overturn a reasonable, but low valuation. A company could be worth 10 million or 15 million, and both are reasonable arguments. The taxpayer has no obligation to inflate the price of his business and give the IRS more money. When he sells his business to his trust, he will sell it for a low but reasonable valuation. The second part of the squeeze involves setting up something called a family limited partnership. It exists to separate management and ownership in a company, and it reduces the taxable value of the company or other assets by anywhere from 10-50 percent. The last part of the process is to pay income taxes out of the grantor's estate; effectively increasing the amount the trust accumulates. This is what the "defect" is in the trust. A long time ago to combat tax avoidance, the IRS decided that certain trusts would create income tax liability for their grantors, to cut down on income splitting. By doing this, they inadvertently opened up a loophole for estate tax planning. What they didn't realize is that this could be used to move money from the grantor's estate to the trust. It works like this. The business earns a million dollars in income, which accrues to the trust. The trust is not considered part of the grantor's estate, but he has to pay income taxes on the trust. He will have to pay the income taxes out of his estate, and the trust will earn tax-free cash. Therefore, the trust earns income, and the grantor pays the taxes. This means that the trust can consume hundreds of millions of dollars from the estate of the grantor, and if the grantor decides it is too much, he is free to begin paying income taxes out of the trust, switching off the "defect". These three techniques show how a business owner with 50 million in assets can avoid paying a dime in estate tax upon transferring his estate.

Business Asset Protection

The first thing to do to protect business assets is to incorporate, if this hasn't been done already. A shocking amount of even successful businesses are run as sole proprietorships or partnerships. LLC incorporation is cheap, easy, and beneficial. The second thing to do is to separate liability into separate businesses. For example, if a person owns 5 rental properties and a business, then they should separate the business from the rental properties, setting up two LLCs. This can be kind of a pain to keep track of all the bank accounts and different corporations, so the way to solve this problem is to form a holding company, known as the master LLC. The fancier way to do it is to set up an asset protection trust as the master company, which is an expensive, but smart choice.

Asset Protection Trusts

What is an Asset Protection Trust (APT)? An Asset Protection Trust is a trust where the person who sets up the trust can also benefit from the trust. They are used by doctors, business owners, and other people with high liability risk. Their purpose is to place assets out of reach of creditors. Nevada is the one of the best states to incorporate an asset protection trust, but the real money is in offshore asset protection trusts, such as Cook Islands trusts. Features of Asset Protection Trust are:

- Spendthrift Clause- This clause prevents beneficiaries from assigning future distributions or borrowing against them.

These are common in trust funds, and they in reality prevent beneficiaries from being sued.

- Irrevocability- This prevents a judge from forcing the grantor of the trust to revoke the trust and hand over the money to the court. You can still retain power to change trustees under most circumstances. You can appoint yourself as "investment consultant" to control how trust assets are invested. You can also use a "letter of wishes" to direct trustee when you don't want to make hard and fast rules on the trust document. Asset protection trustees will tend to be very flexible to your needs and desires.

- Duress Clause- If you have the power to change trustees, this power will normally be taken away from you on days when you have been in court, and will remain out of your reach if there is a judgment entered against you. In reality, it is designed to prevent the court from forcing you to appoint a new trustee, protecting your assets from judgment.

- Discretionary- The trust distributions are not fixed, and sometimes even the beneficiaries of the trust can be changed. In a deposition, for example, you can truthfully say that you have no more interest in the trust than the President of the US, who could also be a beneficiary, but never receive any distributions.

- Flight Clause- Trust can move to another (usually offshore) jurisdiction in the case of trouble.

- Choice of Trustee- Most offshore trusts will have offshore trustees, and the laws of tax havens prohibit them from enforcing orders from foreign courts. Domestic trusts usually rely more on asset protection statutes to throw out cases, rather than ignoring them entirely.

Personal Asset Protection

As I said before, when doing asset protection planning, few assets should be held in the personal name of a smart business owner. The only asset that should be in your name is the bank account you use to pay your daily expenses. It is perfectly acceptable to own vehicles, boats, real estate and other expensive items in a specially designed LLC for them. Cash or credit cards work fine for small purchases of personal property, but the more planning is required for buying larger property, such as cars, boats and planes.

Example—How the mega-rich avoid paying sales tax on yacht and plane purchases

Sales tax is no big deal if you go out to dinner and spend 200 bucks, and end up paying 15-20 bucks or whatever on sales tax. However, sales tax is sometimes worth avoiding, if the items to be bought are large enough. This is especially important for yachts and planes. A million dollar yacht will carry sales tax of over 80 grand in most places. The solution, as always, rests in tax havens and asset protection. There are 7 states with no sales tax, so many, many people register expensive property in the name of a corporation or LLC, and take delivery there too. There are also islands and tax havens with no sales tax, so the boat or plane must be taken for delivery there. This is why most of the world's super yachts carry flags from the places like the British Virgin Islands, Panama, Bermuda, and other tax havens. It saves them a boatload of cash on taxes.

Asset Protection and Divorce

The classic move to protect asset pending marriage is to use a pre-nuptial agreement. However, in some states, like California, courts toss over 50 percent of prenups. They also are notorious for causing fights. However, there is a better solution to protect assets instead. Instead, by setting up an asset protection trust or master LLC structure, you create protection against divorce that is both strong and invisible. This is especially true for people with inherited wealth in equitable distribution states; people in equitable distribution states don't even need a fancy trust for this to work, any trust will do. You don't need anyone's permission to set one of these up. Properly used, this technique should eclipse the prenups.

So far, however, only the wealthiest people have caught on to this method. It is the best of both worlds—effective asset protection for low cost, and no need for complex negotiations before marriage. It also beats the failure rate of the traditional prenups by 95 percent, and is successful 99 percent of the time, even in community property states. Also, the asset protection trust or master LLC structure can be set up if you are already married, subject to the fraudulent transfer provisions of the state you live in, giving protection to those even without any prior planning. Instead of using ineffective and contentious strategies to protect wealth from divorce, use a trust and/or LLC structure.

Avoiding Fraudulent Transfers

Remember from before when we talked about giving stuff away so that creditors are suing you can't get the money? It is called a fraudulent transfer, and it sounds like a crime, but it is in fact, a civil offense, and any such money can be recalled and given to your creditors. The classic example of a fraudulent transfer is giving all your assets away before bankruptcy or divorce, only have

your assets returned afterward. Tax havens tend to require

incredibly high amounts of proof for overturning such transfers

(protecting the debtor), whereas onshore destinations tend to

require less proof (protecting the creditor). Tax havens also typically

don't recognize foreign judgments, have short statutes of limitation,

and use LIFO for trust distributions. All of these factors combine to

make it nearly impossible to get money back once offshore.

Statute of Limitations (from trust setup)
- New York- 6 years
- Nevada- 2 years
- Nevis -18 months
- Cook Islands- 1 year (6 months in some cases)

Burden of Proof
- New York- preponderance (51%)
- Nevada- clear and convincing evidence (80%)
- Nevis/Cook Islands- Beyond a Reasonable doubt (99%).

That's right, it is easier to bring charges for murder in the

Cook Islands than it is to take back someone's money from a Cook

Islands trust. Asset protection, done correctly, is nearly 100 percent effective if done before lawsuits, audits, and other bad things happen to the debtors. Protect assets in times of calm, and you won't risk having a transfer recalled by the UFTA. First of all, if money cannot be found, then it cannot be taken. Also, although the US can put a lot of pressure on a tax haven sheltering terrorists or international criminals, and the havens usually give up those kinds of people, the US federal government technically lacks the jurisdiction to write even a parking ticket in Switzerland, Cayman, or the Cook Islands, and struggles to deal with courts in asset protection friendly states like Nevada, New Hampshire, and Wyoming. Tax havens exist not only to save taxes, but also to protect the assets of wealthy people from their own governments, especially third world governments. Tax haven governments and asset protection friendly US states have laws on the books to protect *debtors,* not the creditors they owe money to.

Summing it up

Wall Street doesn't want you to build wealth; they just want to take your money. Learn their tricks, and don't fall for them. Don't give anyone you don't trust any control of your money, and ask as many questions as you want. You don't have to be intimidated by brokers, advisors, fund managers, and talking heads on television, they just want money to seem complicated so they get more assets. Finance, investing, and trading aren't taught in school, so you need to learn everything you can about them to give yourself the best chance to build wealth. Investing is a good idea over the short and long term. There are great opportunities in stocks, consumer lending, and real estate. Trading is a good opportunity to make big money, but you need to be at the top of your game at all times, and constantly manage risk. Tax laws are written to benefit the wealthy and smart, so take advantage of them. Protect your assets from frivolous lawsuits by using trusts and corporations. Building huge wealth takes time and patience, and hard work will only take you halfway there. Being clever, educated, and working hard will deliver you the

wealth you deserve.

Until next time,
Logan C. Kane

About the Author

Logan C. Kane was born in 1995. He grew up in Loch Lloyd, Missouri, where he took an early interest in investing and trading. He invested money for several clients in Loch Lloyd, making each investor a profit. To this day, he has never lost money for a client. He attended The Barstow School in Kansas City, where he often traded stocks during study hall– and class. He then attended the University of Miami, receiving a Presidential scholarship. He attended there for one year before dropping out due to health issues. Inspired by overcoming his health challenges, he personally financed a wish in 2016 for an ill child in Miami, paying for him to meet Ryan Tannehill. He generously supports the Make-a-Wish foundation and the Leukemia Lymphoma society. In his free time, he enjoys spending time with family, traveling, and sports. He continues to invest today, taking a more conservative approach and earning steady profits. This is his first book.

CPSIA information can be obtained
at www.ICGtesting.com
Printed in the USA
FSHW021315230119
55210FS

9 781520 250366